SOME ENGLISH
SYMPHONISTS

SOME ENGLISH SYMPHONISTS

A SELECTION FROM
ESSAYS IN MUSICAL ANALYSIS

BY

DONALD FRANCIS TOVEY

OXFORD UNIVERSITY PRESS
LONDON NEW YORK TORONTO
1941

OXFORD UNIVERSITY PRESS
AMEN HOUSE, E.C. 4
London Edinburgh Glasgow New York
Toronto Melbourne Capetown Bombay
Calcutta Madras
HUMPHREY MILFORD
PUBLISHER TO THE UNIVERSITY

PRINTED IN GREAT BRITAIN

CONTENTS

ELGAR

'Falstaff', Symphonic Study, Op. 68 7
Violoncello Concerto in E Minor, Op. 85 . . . 20
Violin Concerto in B minor, Op. 61 23
Variations for Orchestra, Op. 35 29
Overture, 'Cockaigne', Op. 40 32
Symphony in E flat, No. 2, Op. 63 34
Concert Overture, 'In the South' (Alassio), Op. 50 . . 41
Introduction and Allegro for Strings (Quartet and Orchestra),
    Op. 47 45

VAUGHAN WILLIAMS

Concerto Accademico, in D minor, for Violin and String
    Orchestra 48
Pastoral Symphony. 51
Overture to 'The Wasps' 55

ARTHUR SOMERVELL

Violin Concerto in G minor 57
'Normandy': Symphonic Variations for Pianoforte with
    Orchestra 63

WILLIAM WALTON

Viola Concerto 67

C. HUBERT H. PARRY

Symphonic Variations for Orchestra 73
'Overture to an Unwritten Tragedy' 76

PREFACE

TWENTY-FIVE essays in the six volumes of *Essays in Musical Analysis* are concerned with orchestral works by British composers. That this by no means represents the total of the native music performed by the Reid Orchestra, which Professor Tovey founded in 1916 and directed till his death in 1940, is explained in the preface to Volume II (1935).

The Reid Orchestra has produced fully twice as many contemporary works as appear in these volumes; not that that amounts to much. In several cases I have been able to obtain the composer's own analysis which, however modestly expressed, has an authority to which I obviously cannot claim, though I have sometimes intervened in footnotes when the composer's modesty has been actually misleading.

Tovey particularly regretted that he had had no opportunity of writing an analysis for Bantock's Hebridean Symphony, 'a work which is on its way to becoming hackneyed for the Reid Orchestra', because in this he was forestalled by 'Bantock's friend and biographer, H. Osmond Anderton'. It may be regretted here that his series of Elgar's symphonic works were never completed with the Symphony No. 1 in A flat. It is fortunate, however, that he did not know of Elgar's own commentary on 'Falstaff' (*Musical Times*, 1913) in time to be deterred from writing a full analysis himself. Such knowledge might have deprived us of the masterly essay which begins this volume.

The sixteen essays here collected together are the most important of the twenty-five which show the author's mind towards his contemporary countrymen. Their choice is based on the importance of the essay rather than of the work, and it must be remembered that the choice was determined by the requirements of the Reid Orchestra's programmes, not by the author's own taste. In the same preface he declares:

'I emphatically decline to be judged by the modern works which I have *not* yet produced and analysed.'

1941   H. C. C.

ELGAR

'FALSTAFF', SYMPHONIC STUDY, OP. 68

Since I wrote this analysis the composer kindly gave me permission to correct it by comparison with his own commentary, which appeared in *The Musical Times* of September 1st, 1913, and which, to my shame, I had not read. But my delinquency has its advantages; for it gives rise to a unique opportunity for demonstrating how far a great piece of 'programme music' can be intelligible as pure music and at the same time convey the subject of the composer's illustration to other minds without the use of words. Accordingly I have retained my analysis with all its mistakes, and have corrected it by the composer's analysis in footnotes marked (E). This initial must not be taken to make the composer responsible for the wording of the footnotes; but it implies his authority for their substance. On the whole I am quite satisfied with my success in guessing the composer's literary meaning. Glaring failure about main points would be as unsatisfactory from the composer's point of view as from mine; for my impressions are those of a musician, and not those of a dilettante who might be excused for all manner of blunders in appraising musical values. Where I am wrong I do not see how I could have guessed right, but I have no difficulty in seeing the composer's point when his account corrects me.

Prophecy about the judgement of posterity is as otiose a game in matters of art as in other matters of history. But I have sometimes been compelled to investigate works of art that I should not care to revive; and I have never found in a perishable work anything like the signs of greatness and vitality that abound in Elgar's *Falstaff*. How its musical values can ever diminish I cannot see. To prove the greatness of a work of art is a task as hopeless as it would be tedious; but, like the candidate who failed in geometry, I think I can make the greatness of this one appear highly probable.

Let me begin by 'blowing the expense', and for once giving a tolerably complete list of thematic quotations. With thirty-three musical examples I have to omit any theme or incident that does not recur outside its first context; hence, any theme that appears only or always in continuity with a quoted theme, and any variation that can be described in words or easily recognized on a first hearing. Even so, I could describe several passages more easily with the aid of another six quotations.

This enormous mass of definitely different themes is about equal to that of Beethoven's Eroica or Ninth Symphony; and Elgar's work is one continuous movement, not essentially interrupted by its two intermezzi. It is completely independent of the Lisztian doctrine that all the themes of a symphonic poem should be derivable from a single thematic cell or *Urkeim*. The plausibility of that doctrine lies in the fact that a ripe and highly intellectual musical style tends to develop fascinating thematic connexions as a form of wit. The fatal weakness of the doctrine is that such wit does not concern the foundations of musical composition at all, and is not necessarily more logical than a series of puns. Speaking without the composer's correction, I see and hear no musical reason why these thirty-three quotations should prove to have any thematic relations beyond those to which I draw attention. But in the art of composition the work coheres like a diamond. Its clarity is the crystalline artistic simplicity that comes from the enormous pressures of an inexhaustible imagination; not from the weary eliminations of a taste that declines from one boredom to the next. It is not a matter of previously ascertained form; nor is it a matter of literary illustration.

To the task of musical illustration Elgar brings the resources of a mind long ago well and deeply read, and especially replenished for the matter in hand. He is of the classical race of *attentive* artists; his view of his literary subject will be intensely his own, because his mind will be concentrated upon it. Hence his musical illustrations will amount to a close symbolical tissue, like those by which Bach, Mozart, and Beethoven habitually illustrate words when illustration is called for. Nevertheless I do not propose to analyse *Falstaff* from this point of view. I know neither this music nor the two parts of *King Henry the Fourth* well enough to do so; and in the nature of the case the music is (as Mendelssohn urged in a very profound argument on musical illustration) much more definite than words. And it so happens that Shakespeare has not given Sir John to us in a connected narrative at all, but in a series of episodes deftly but by no means closely wrought into an historic pageant, which is another series of episodes with little more coherence than that of popular history. But, strange to say, it is just in the management of such pageantry that the capacity for composition is most severely tested. Elgar's *Falstaff* is as close and inevitable a musical structure as anything since Beethoven; and this cannot be claimed for *Henry the Fourth*. But for *Henry the Fourth*, alike in the aspects of comedy, chronicle, and tragedy, it can be claimed that Shakespeare's power of movement is at its height; in other words, that the art of composition is omnipresent in that general sense which is more vital than any external form. And here Elgar's power is identical with Shakespeare's, and, being subject to none but purely musical conditions that are its own breath of life, it also achieves a perfect external form. One of the essential characteristics of that form is the combination of weighty symphonic development with episodic leisure and freedom. I hope to show, as occasion arises, how vividly the composer brings before us, by sheer power of abstract form, the contrast between the irresponsible roisterings of the comedians and the ominous background of dynastic troubles.

But I am not going to look for minute details. The particular illustrations I can at present see are obvious enough. I should not be surprised to learn that there were hundreds more; but the composer has not lost grasp of his music in their pursuit, and you and I certainly will lose grasp of the music if we do not attend exclusively to it. When we know both Elgar's and Shakespeare's Falstaff by heart we may amuse ourselves with Gadshill robberies and the arithmetical progression of rogues in buckram. Till then let us be broadly general over the human characters, and attentively musical about details and forms. (By the way, I take it that *The Merry Wives of Windsor* may be neglected. The composer who wishes to put Falstaff into an opera must use *The Merry Wives of Windsor* as the only possible framework of a plot; but the real Falstaff is not there except in one or two good phrases.) Here is unquestionably the real Falstaff, wallowing, protesting, and formidable in his absurdity.[1]

No doubt it may be possible to find the Shakespearian origin of the following pair of satellite themes; but all I know is that one is perky or quizzical, like any Elizabethan page—

and the other scolding, like some aspects of Mistress Quickly[2] or less respectable persons (overleaf).

---

[1] Not as yet quite absurd but (as Morgann says, writing in 1777) 'in a green old age, mellow, frank, gay, easy, corpulent, loose, unprincipled, and luxurious'. (E.)

[2] Exx. 2 and 3 are among Falstaff's personal themes. 'I am not only witty in myself, but the cause that wit is in others.' (E.)

Ex. 3.

But the later developments of these themes do not fit any particulars of the kind, and Ex. 2 is no subordinate character in the whole work. A counterstatement gives Ex. 1 in the bass below a cataract of trills into which the scoldings have merged. One of the most significant features of style in this work is the fact that most of the themes will make powerful basses, as already shown at the outset by the fact that Ex. 1 stands without harmony. In this respect Elgar may remind us of Richard Strauss, especially as something like the Straussian *panache* is essential to the character of Falstaff. But, with all respect to Strauss, there is more art in *Falstaff* than in *Ein Heldenleben*. The unaccompanied main theme of *Heldenleben* is great; but the problem of its eventual harmonization is contemptuously evaded, whereas Elgar's harmonization never suggests that it was ever a problem at all, whether it consists of a combination of themes or a mass of impressionist scoring. And every one of Elgar's combinations of themes is a statement of excellent harmony made by the combined melodies. The more modern view regards the technical difficulty of this as a restraint. The wiser view recognizes it as a resource. A student with a dangerous sense of humour once brought to my score-playing class some pages of *Falstaff* as a prepared task. He forestalled my comments by explaining that being pressed for time, he had chosen these pages as a 'soft option' because, though for full orchestra, they consisted entirely of two-part harmony. This satisfies Brahms's test with a vengeance, the test of covering up the middle of the score in order to see what the top and bottom is worth 'without trimmings'.

In the fourth theme of the opening complex we clearly recognize Prince Hal in the mood[1] of that soliloquy when he declares his intention of imitating the sun by allowing himself to be hidden in base contagious clouds in order to be more wondered at when he breaks through them.

Ex. 4.

This theme is noble; and the composer would have gone wrong in his musical and dramatic psychology if he had made it otherwise. Breeding will tell, whatever flaws may deface the character. But

[1] In his most courtly and genial mood. The symbol of his stern military character will be found in Ex. 28 of the present essay. (E.)

Elgar withholds his accolade; this theme is *not* marked *nobilmente*, though that is how it must be played. It is true to the Shakespearian irony, deeper than the Sophoclean, and perhaps less aware of itself than the Euripidean; true to the irony which indulges in popular sentiments with apparent zest until the very groundlings must feel the approach of shame. Shylock and the glorious sport of Jew-baiting; Hamlet and the diverting farce of lunacy; Prince Hal, who owes Falstaff his love, and who has from first to last been stealing the pleasures of disreputable 'ragging' with the deliberate intention of pompously and publicly disgracing his poor dupes as soon as he is crowned; all these things the interpreter of Shakespeare should give us with the illusory side foremost. The poet's deeper views may be subversive, but the uneasy censor will discover nothing but impenetrable popular orthodoxy.

The continuation of Ex. 4 is broadly melodious and based on different material which I do not quote. Its counterstatement is followed by a re-entry of Ex. 1 in violas with a sinuous counterpoint in the 'cellos. Suddenly it turns aside into the remote key of E minor, where a new theme appears.

Ex. 5.

scherzando.

Except in obvious cases, I do not propose to identify themes with persons. But we may go so far as to identify bass registers with male characters. And Ex. 5 lends itself to stratagems and spoils.[1] It is given time to explain itself in square statements and counter-statements. Then the perky-and-scolding complex (Exx. 2 and 3) returns and leads to a grand peroration reviewing all the themes and unobtrusively introducing a new tottering bass to Falstaff.

Ex. 6.

The peroration ends with a descent of Ex. 1 from the top of the orchestra to the bass register of the last bars of the theme. These are reiterated expectantly, with a pause.[2] Now, in a quicker tempo,

---

[1] The rising scale in the latter part of this quotation shows Falstaff as cajoling and persuasive. (E.)

[2] Thus far Section 1, presenting Falstaff and Prince Henry. (E.)

action begins.[1] Still we have to deal with new themes, and not until the fat is in the fire (as might be Falstaff larding the lean earth at Gadshill) do the new themes combine with the old.

First we have a group of four new figures conspiring together in a single sentence.

Ex. 7.

Ex. 8.

Ex. 9.

Ex. 10.[2]

These are repeated with a new modulation after a pause. A new theme impinges on them, blown up like a bladder with sighing and grief.[3]

Ex. 11.

It is given plenty of room to vent its grievance; and then the action begins. Both the figures of Ex. 6 are developed in a fugato in combination with Exx. 1 and 5. This quickly leads to a collapse upon Ex. 7, which is thrice insisted on. Then the figures of Exx. 8 and 9 conclude this exposition.

At the present juncture, whatever events may have been so far represented they issue now in a noble outburst of Falstaffian moral indignation.

[1] Section II. Eastcheap—Gadshill—The Boar's Head, revelry, and sleep. (E.)

[2] Women, such as the Hostess, Doll Tearsheet, and 'a dozen or fourteen honest gentlewomen'. (E.)

[3] Not at all! 'A goodly, portly man, of a cheerful look, a pleasing eye, and a most noble carriage.' (E.)

Ex. 12.[1]

Harmonized grandly in two-part counterpoint, relieved from austerity by occasional faintly heard inner notes, this theme, like many others in the work, is exposed in the manner of a fugue. There are three entries: soprano, alto, and bass. It is important to realize, as Bradley points out, that Falstaff is no coward, either in fact or in reputation. In battle Sir John Coleville surrendered to him on the strength of his name. The object of Poins in the Gadshill plot was to show him up not as a coward but as a boaster. Poins clearly distinguishes him from his two colleagues thus:

'Well, for two of them, I know them to be as true-bred cowards as ever turned back; and for the third, if he fight longer than he sees reason, I'll forswear arms.'

Honour hath no skill in surgery, and Falstaff will tolerate no humbug but himself. I ask the reader to glance ahead to Ex. 17 for the magnificent combination of Exx. 12 and 11, which here follows in a lower key, less convenient for printing in an economical way. Ex. 11 is then continued in combination with the quaver figure of Ex. 7. With a rapid decrescendo the music recedes into distance, and the conspirators, Exx. 7, 8, 9, now plot in whispers. Falstaff (Ex. 1 broken up in a variation alternately with the figure of Ex. 9) is alert but mystified. Something new and innocent makes its appearance.[2]

Ex. 13.

But I am afraid that the Prince is also tiptoeing in the neighbourhood with mischievous intent—

Ex. 14. Outline of Ex. 4.

and though Falstaff in 'diminution' does not seem formidable, I would not trust him with my money.

---

[1] 'I am a rogue if I were not at half sword with a dozen of them two hours together.' (E.)

[2] A cheerful out-of-door ambling theme. (E.)

Ex. 15.   Ex. 1 diminished.

As this mysterious episode develops, the connexion between Ex. 13 and Ex. 4 becomes more obvious. Ex. 12 persists quietly in its course, with evident effort to maintain its nonchalance. But the surrounding darkness is too much for it, and eventually all themes are lost in a passage consisting of ominous rustlings and whisperings. Prince Hal, in a new variation anticipating Ex. 16, is present; another conspirator (Ex. 5, Falstaff himself?)[1] is groaning in the background. The ominous rustlings are resumed with deeper tone; but they suddenly end in a sportive version of Prince Hal's theme, accompanied by running triplets.

Ex. 16.   Variation of Ex. 4.

This is given room to display itself thrice in different keys. Then shrill cries and whistles[2] lead to a fierce fight. Ex. 12, diminished in quavers, hacks its fugal way in A minor with the utmost energy,[3] and soon settles down in E minor to reiterating its first figure with growing emphasis, until it merges into a re-entry of Ex. 10, loud, complaining, and, as before, soon combining grandly with Ex. 11 at its full size, thus—

Ex. 17.

Suddenly this dies away, and Ex. 7, with both its figures, expresses unholy glee in dialogue between various treble instruments. A new theme of syncopated minim chords,

appears softly and timidly above tambourine-sounds of marching steps. At a sudden stand-and-deliver, Ex. 13 reappears, at first with a new full-toned boldness, but it fades out into Ex. 11, plangent as ever, though faint, on muted horns below derisive scales descending in the violins. Falstaff also bestirs himself in diminution (as in Ex. 15), perhaps a little testy under the persistent and monotonous gibes of Ex. 10.

[1] Yes; see note on Ex. 5.
[2] The short struggle for the twice-stolen booty 'got with much ease'. (E.)   [3] The discomfiture of the thieves. (E.)

And now comes one of the most remarkable features in the form of this work. In and around the key of G minor, Ex. 10 occupies no less than fifty-eight bars, thirty-two of which are marked to be repeated.[1] Nothing breaks the monotony of two-bar rhythm, and there are not many breaks in the series of 4-bar or even 8-bar phrases in which the episode runs its course. As with the stiff, antithetic style of Schumann, the interest lies largely in epigrammatic wit. Elgar has temperamentally much in common with Schumann, and at any time in his career he could have made himself as popular as Grieg by abandoning all methods of composition except the rigid mosaic of Schumann's larger works. But such a style ceases to be rigid and becomes a mighty achievement of athletic muscle when it is absorbed into the contrasts of a freely organized work. This episode has, in relation to the rest, exactly the audacity of movement by which Shakespeare carries us through the several scenes in which Prince Hal is wasting unlimited time with his pot-house companions. Among details, notice the combination of Exx. 10 and 5, classically euphonious like all Elgar's counterpoint.

At length Falstaff protests. The solo Falstaff of the orchestra, the bassoon, almost as loud as Coleridge thought it to be, declaims in terms of Ex. 12, *quasi recitativo*. It collapses cynically into Ex. 9, out of which arises a new theme in the chattering staccato of the wood-wind.

Ex. 18.

The composition still maintains its sectional, episodic character while this new theme, together with a complaining, slow chromatic counterpoint, develops into a row. When this has run its course and died away, the former badinage is recapitulated with an effect of insolent regularity, though it is really only epitomized. But it includes Ex. 12 again, although Falstaff's voice, worn out in the singing of anthems, becomes alarmingly wheezy. Soon we hear him sleeping. And though the musical illustration of this is as audible as sleep can be, it reveals, both in itself and in its context, the poetic depth of the whole work. A mere musical illustrator would, even if he failed to show why Falstaff was in hiding behind the arras, certainly have tried to illustrate the exposition of the contents of Falstaff's pockets, and the derision aroused by the famous bill for a ha'porth of bread with an intolerable deal of sack. But the more we study Elgar's Falstaff the clearer does it appear

---

[1] The 'honest gentlewomen's' theme, now complete and raised to due importance, runs its scherzo-like course. (E.)

that the composer is achieving something lofty, severe, consistent, and far out of the depth of opera or even of drama. He is giving us Falstaff entirely from Falstaff's own point of view. The old rascal is not sentimental; but, as Theobald divined from a corrupt text, ' 'a babbled of green fields' on his death-bed; and Elgar knows that when he slept there was a wistful beauty in his dreams of Jack Falstaff, a boy who could have crept into any alderman's thumb-ring, page to the Duke of Norfolk.

The theme of the 'Dream Interlude' has a purposely indefinite family resemblance to such quizzicalities as Ex. 9; but not even the thread of personality itself can make a solid bridge over the gulf between that dreamland past and the drastic present.[1]

Ex. 19.

Falstaff awakes again to his roistering world.[2] Exx. 2-3 return in full vigour. And now he must play the soldier. I hazard the guess that in the following new complex of themes we may perhaps see Falstaff as recruiting officer, and can agree with his estimate of his mouldy, feeble, warty, and vituline recruits.

Ex. 20.

Ex. 21.[3]

Ex. 22.[4]

Between Ex. 21 and Ex. 22 the contrapuntal combination of Ex. 10 over Ex. 5 intervenes. I know nothing more 'gravity-removing' than the effect of Ex. 22 when it is delivered timidly in musical dumb-crambo by the various thumpers and tinklers known as the 'kitchen' department of the orchestra.

[1] The contrast of 'what might have been'. (E.)
[2] Section III. Falstaff's March—The return through Gloucestershire—The new king—The hurried ride to London. (E.)
[3] A fanfare, once distant, then nearer. (E.)
[4] A fitting accompaniment to the marching gait of the scarecrow army. (E.)

Another theme joins the slouching march and initiates a fugato which gradually develops into a fight (without prejudice to the etymological connexion of fugue and flight).

Ex. 23.[1]

There is also evidence of what Bradley calls 'so ridiculous an object as Falstaff running'. (Combination of Exx. 1 and 6.) But such absurdity, Bradley also implies, is immune, and Falstaff gains credit in battle by frauds which show effrontery rather than cowardice. There are a few more new figures in this battle episode (if such it be), but they do not recur, and the tumult soon dies away. With extraordinary subtlety Ex. 22 becomes a new formal lyric episode, in alternation with Ex. 23.

Ex. 24.[2]

Then, as if the land were once more safe for wayfarers, we renew our acquaintance with Ex. 13, in alternation with a new rustic and reedy motive of laziness.

Ex. 25.

And so we come to Shallow's orchard, where, in another self-contained episode, we listen to tabor and pipe—

Ex. 26.

and indulge in drowsy reminiscences.

Ex. 27.

[1] The March. 'I have foundered nine score and odd posts.' (E.)
[2] As we approach the fields and apple-trees the march assumes a song-like character. (E.)

This interlude comes to a definite end: but the drowsy motive of Ex. 26 would fain continue. It is rudely interrupted by a shrill outburst of violins (another new figure), reintroducing Ex. 8. 'Under which king, Bezonian? Speak or die?' Harry the Fifth's the man; and we shall all be augmented in the new fount of honour. (Ex. 12 by augmentation. No extra marks will be awarded to candidates who detect this point.) Exx. 23 and 22 scurry away post-haste into the distance.

After a pause we find ourselves near Westminster Abbey amid solemn sounds betokening the approach of the coronation procession.[1] A new theme—

Ex. 28.

sounds a note of insistent appeal. As it eventually proves to be Falstaff's last death-bed gesture, I presume that it indicates his passionate belief[2] that the king will be to him the beloved prince glorified. Laughter is in the air—

Ex. 29.

and, in another new theme, Falstaff shares in the glow of affectionate loyalty to the new king.

Ex. 30.

(This immediately combines in counterpoint with Ex. 1.) Another theme may be taken to be at least consistent with cheers and the waving of caps.

Ex. 31.

Poor Falstaff still believes that Henry the Fifth is the light fantastic Hal of Ex. 16. So that brilliant variation is the substance of the

---

[1] Section IV. King Henry V's progress.—The repudiation of Falstaff, and his death.

[2] No. It is the King himself in military character. (E.)

next crescendo, and Falstaff's cheers transform Ex. 31 to its rhythm.

Ex. 32.

The king arrives in all his glory (Ex. 4, *grandioso*, for Elgar still will not say *nobilmente*). The cheers are loud, but there is a barrier between the king and his old friends.

Ex. 33.

Falstaff's heart is fracted and corroborate: the joyful whoop at the end of Ex. 28 becomes a bewildered question, and nothing is left for him but disillusioned memories. The rest is easy for the listener to follow, there are no new themes, and the long tale of old themes is given in the form of reminiscence, not development. Here is the tale: Ex. 28 last figure, Ex. 5; pause; Ex. 28 revived; Exx. 12, 5, 21,[1] 31, 33, subsiding into a mournful decline on the subject of Ex. 28; a faint echo of Ex. 33, then the laughter of Ex. 29 at half pace, transformed as if to falling tears; failing memories of Exx. 7, 1, and 5: a long pause; a breath of sleep-laden wind from Shallow's orchard, Ex. 27, disturbed for a moment by the quizzical accent of Ex. 10, now heard for the last time; it melts into pathos, and Ex. 27 declines farther into an entirely unspoilt memory of the prince whom Falstaff loved (Ex. 4, in full, pianissimo and cantabile); then Ex. 1, failing.[2] Mistress Quickly's account of his death is neither more nor less pathetic than Elgar's; but here, as throughout the work, Elgar is giving us Falstaff's own mind, which is far beyond the comprehension of any other character in the play. We may perhaps recognize Mistress Quickly in a mournful cadence of the clarinet just after the fading out of Ex. 1; but up to the last we cannot be sure that we are spectators: the sudden final rally on Ex. 28, with its bold presentment of the remote key of E minor as penultimate to the last chord, will do equally well for a salute from Falstaff to his estranged king,[3] or as an epitaph in praise of his

---

[1] It is the furious fanfare of Ex. 21 which marks the King's sentence of banishment. (E.)

[2] The moment of death is marked here by a full chord of C major pianissimo on the brass. (E.)

[3] The King's stern theme thrown curtly across the picture. (E.)

loyalty. He was a soldier, and, with all his humbug, no coward; so let him go to Arthur's bosom with a roll of muffled drums.[1]

It will not surprise me to learn that every one of my parallels between the music and the particulars of Falstaff's doings and surroundings is wrong, except the illustration of his snoring. About such sounds there can be no mistake; snores are snores whether they are produced by double-basses and a contrafagotto or by the nose; and if the composer does not mean them he ought not to produce them. But I have hopes that this analysis may not be misleading as to the musical form and Shakespeare-Elgar psychology of the work as a whole.

VIOLONCELLO CONCERTO IN E MINOR, OP. 85

1 *Adagio, introductory to Moderato, leading to* 2 *Allegro molto.*
3 *Adagio, leading to* 4 *a recitative, leading to*
5 *Allegro ma non troppo.*

Although the musical language of this work is unaffectedly classical, its forms are unlike those of any other concerto; conspicuously unlike, for instance, the elaborate classical design of Elgar's Violin Concerto. The Violoncello Concerto is a fairy-tale, full, like all Elgar's larger works, of meditative and intimate passages; full also of humour, which, in the second movement and finale, rises nearer to the surface than Elgar usually permits. Though the work is highly organized, an elaborate analysis is not necessary so long as enough themes are quoted. Lucidity is the aim and the achievement of its form and style; not the thin mundane lucidity of a Saint-Saëns concerto, nor yet the arrogant lucidity of the epigrammatist who has not got over his famous discovery of the stupidity of most people.

Mutatis mutandis, this violoncello concerto well represents its composer's Schumannesque mood. This term will seem grotesque to those numerous musicians to whom orchestration is the *sine qua non* of musical thought; but Schumann's helplessness in that category rather reveals than conceals the shyness that goes with such intimate moods. The shyness is, however, just as compatible with consummate mastery of the orchestra; and indeed Elgar's orchestration is as unworldly as it is masterly. In the Violoncello Concerto

[1] No: the drum roll is shrill; the man of stern reality has triumphed.

the orchestra is throughout concentrated on the special task of throwing into relief a solo instrument which normally lies below the surface of the harmony. Brilliant orchestration is thus out of the question; but there is no lack of subtle and beautiful tone-colour, inexhaustibly varied within narrow limits and by the simplest means.

After a short recitative-like introduction by the violoncello—

the first movement begins with an indolent sequential theme, announced unharmonized by the violas—

and repeated by the violoncello. The movement is not in sonata form, but is a simple lyric design with a middle section in 12/8 time. This is introduced by the following theme—

which then blossoms out into the major mode thus—

There is a free recapitulation of the main section (Ex. 2). Then, after a momentary allusion to the introduction (Ex. 1), the second movement, a lively scherzo in G major, begins tentatively with the following figure:

This soon gathers speed and seems about to work itself out, with a few other themes, as a free sonata-form movement, with a second subject beginning in the remote key of E flat, which, however, it soon abandons.

Ex. 6.

largamente   a tempo.

Having produced just enough effect of development to take us beyond lyric forms, the impish little movement scurries back to its G major and vanishes with the detonation of a burst bubble.

The serene slow movement, in B flat (the Ultima Thule from E minor, the key of the concerto), is a single broad melody. For future reference I number its first two phrases separately.

Ex. 7.

Adagio.

Ex. 8.

&c.

The movement ends on the dominant, with its first phrase (as in Ex. 7), and thus leads into the introduction to the finale. This introduction begins in B flat minor, with an adumbration of the future main theme, which is turned by the violoncello into a recitative not unlike that at the beginning of the concerto. The finale then begins, in full swing.

Ex. 9.

It is a free rondo, with a mischievous second subject, slightly suggestive of dignity at the mercy of a banana-skin.

Ex. 10.

allargando.   a tempo.

f dolce.   p   f   sf

The movement is spaciously developed on a large scale, with many and varied episodes. A complete surprise awaits us towards the end in a new slow theme of romantically abstruse harmony and full of pathos.

The metre, already new, changes to 3/4, where yet another fresh theme—

rises to a climax of passion, thence to subside into the second strain of the slow movement (Ex. 8), and from that to the opening of the concerto (Ex. 1). Then the main theme of the finale works up tersely to a spirited and abrupt end.

VIOLIN CONCERTO IN B MINOR, OP. 61

1 *Allegro.* 2 *Andante.* 3 *Allegro molto.*

Elgar's Violin Concerto, like the *Enigma Variations*, and probably like many other of its composer's finest inspirations, is a character study. This is attested by its dedication to some one unnamed, in the words prefaced in the score: '*Aquí está encerrada el alma de* ... (1910).'

Of all external subjects for music the illustration of human character is the most purely musical; if indeed it can be an external subject at all. Music either has character, or it is meaningless, and the character either has human interest or none. We nourish our interest in the characters of animals by describing them in human terms; and if there is such a thing as 'cosmic emotion', it is nourished by contrasting the vastness of the universe with the insignificance of man, while at the same time we pride ourselves in the fact that it is the human mind which recognizes the contrast. The blank space which stands for the name of the person whose soul is enshrined in this concerto shows that nothing is to be gained by inquiring into the private affairs of Sir Edward Elgar and his friends. The soul of the music is musical, and we need no further external programme. My analysis, therefore, will have nothing but musical facts to present to the listener. I give as nearly as possible a complete list of the themes, a policy which saves many a difficult paragraph of description. But the quotations, though numerous, are very short; and the listener will be grievously misled if he infers from this that the melodies represented by them are short. There is in fact the same danger here as there is in the orthodox discussion of Wagnerian leitmotiv, and such famous examples of the use of an all-pervading figure as the first movement of Beethoven's C minor Symphony; the danger that the analysis may ignore the flowing paragraph in its fascinated study of the pregnant word. When such one-sided analysis is made a basis for the teaching of composition, the results may be paralysing or destructive; and there are such things as compositions that have no flow and no real coherence, because the composer has been deceived into believing that a composition can be built upwards from single figures, 'logically' connected by a process which has little more logic in it than a series of puns.

The following fifteen quotations are, then, no more than the first words or leading words of the paragraphs and the processes which they initiate. I quote them thus briefly, not because the melodies are short, but because there are so many different long melodies and long processes based on the same figures that it is convenient to quote their common factors. If this work were a Wagnerian opera, nothing would be easier than to label one pair of bars the motive of longing, and another the motive of ambition, and to imagine that the composer and the dramatist were both equally capable of designing a dramatic scene by permutations and combinations of some twenty such motives and titles, each consisting of six or seven such highly significant notes that the initiated listener is miraculously certain of their meaning. Such a doctrine would not be worth refuting, but for the fact that composers themselves have been misled by it. This concerto refutes it triumphantly. I have heard it admired for the shortness of its themes, and I have heard it blamed for its lack of broad melodies. The answer to the equally mistaken admiration and blame is already to be found in the fact that the first paragraph is an entirely straightforward matter containing three distinct and important themes.

Ex. 1.

Ex. 2.

Ex. 3.

Even so it is not quite complete, but closes into the next paragraph, which works out, in broad melodious sequences of urgent character, a new theme announced in a darker key.

Ex. 4.

The next theme is destined, later on, to express a serene calm—

Ex. 5.

but the modulations to which it here gives rise, lead quickly to an excited climax in an extremely remote key, with a new figure closely allied to Ex. 2.

Ex. 6.

This swings round in five bars back to B minor, where we have Ex. 4 in an inner part below new counterpoints, followed by a further development of Exx. 1 and 2. So far we have heard nothing of the solo violin. What we have been listening to is a fine modern example of the classical opening tutti of a concerto. These six themes have been welded together in a continuous flow of melody. The changes of key, though more remote and more frequent than those of any older concerto, have all been changes possible in a flow of melody; they have not been events marked off from each other by dramatic action. The master who is to hold this large orchestra spell-bound, and set all these themes out on their various different planes, has not yet spoken. We have now reached the moment when the orchestra is eagerly awaiting him. The strings speak of him wistfully, as in the two bars represented by Ex. 1. Their sentence is finished for them by the master himself.

This entry of the solo violin realizes in a new way the true relation between the solo and the orchestra in the classical concerto form. After a short but broadly ruminating recitative, the violin, passing through Ex. 2, discusses Ex. 4 with the orchestra. Then Ex. 3 (which, by the way, is obviously closely allied to Ex. 1) is developed through a wide range of keys as a rich transition passage, drifting slowly but surely, with the aid of its ally Ex. 6, to G major. In this key Ex. 5 now blossoms out as a broadly lyric second subject. After this has been given free expression we are surprised for a moment by the appearance of Ex. 1 in its original key, a phenomenon which, however, does not mean a return to the tonic, inasmuch as one of the subtleties of the opening tutti was that its first chords were ambiguous in key. Thus the oracle proves its tragic infallibility, for the key turns out to be F sharp minor, the dominant minor. Ex. 4 is worked up, with various derivatives from Ex. 1, and a new counterpoint from the solo violin, to a great climax in which Ex. 3 also plays its part; until at last the full orchestra crashes in with an impassioned tutti beginning with Ex. 4 and passing through remote keys with a still more impassioned development of what was once the calm lyric strain of Ex. 5. Ex. 1 joins powerfully in the stormy dialogue and soon brings the development round to the original key.

Suddenly the storm subsides, and the solo violin re-enters, completing the half-spoken word of the orchestra as on its first entry, but with a quite new meaning, while muted horns murmur the rhythm of the first bar of Ex. 4. The effect is quite clearly that of a return to a recapitulation; and what now follows has all the manner thereof. In actual fact it is very free. The main theme of the second subject (Ex. 5), for instance, appears almost at once below the meditative florid figures of the solo violin, and executes some beautiful remote modulations before the violin resumes the transition themes, Exx. 4, 3, and their accessories. It then appears again in sequences that recall its tentative appearance in the opening tutti; and when at last it settles down to a real feeling of recapitulation its key is not the tonic, but D major. This establishes the same balance of keys that Schubert has in his Unfinished Symphony; but as the original course of Elgar's second subject swerved from G major to the dominant F sharp minor, it now has to take a different direction to swing round from D major to B minor, the main key. This it effects with more sombre dramatic force than before; the entry of the brass being particularly impressive where the violin resumes the discussion of Ex. 4 in B minor. From this point the coda grafts itself on to the recapitulation, and, with the impetuous intervention of Ex. 2, brings the movement to its impassioned end with the first theme, Ex. 1, and its variant, Ex. 3.

The slow movement is in the extremely remote key of B flat. There is something quaint in the fact that two modern violin concertos which are almost at opposite poles of artistic outlook should both be in B minor, and both have this exceptional key relationship in their slow movements. Of Saint-Saëns's third Violin Concerto it may be said without offence that it is all publicity, whereas Elgar's Violin Concerto is one of the most intimate works of this century. In most respects the comparison between the two works sheds little light on either of them, but it is interesting to compare the most obvious single feature in the slow movement of each. Everybody who remembers the slow movement of Saint-Saëns's B minor Violin Concerto instantly thinks of the passage where the violin plays arpeggios in harmonics two octaves above a clarinet. Everybody who remembers the slow movement of the Elgar Violin Concerto thinks of the way in which the orchestra first states eight bars of naïve melody, whereupon the solo violin enters with an equally naïve counterpoint *as an inner part*.

Ex. 7.
Solo.
Orchestra.

Soon the violin leads the orchestra into remote regions; and new themes appear—

Ex. 8.

Ex. 9.
(⌒)

which rise to a climax in D flat.

Ex. 10.
f

In this key the first theme (Ex. 7 with its counterpoint) is resumed, and leads through Ex. 8 to a broad new theme in D natural.

Ex. 11.

&c.

This, though it sets out very firmly in D, does not remain there long but fetches a compass quickly back to B flat, where, with the

return to the main theme, we also have other themes freely recapitulated in their order. The last words are said by the orchestra
with Ex. 10 pianissimo, answered by the violin with Ex. 9.

The finale is very rhapsodical and dramatic. Its outstanding
features are an opening in which the solo violin seems to be playing
a kind of prelude on a figure of rising turns. This requires no
quotation until an inner part of the orchestra interpolates a theme
which afterwards becomes important.

Ex. 12.

This appears to be a determining point, inasmuch as it brings the
harmony to the crisis of closing in the key of B minor, which all this
improvisatorial opening is intended to establish. It is obviously
right that after the slow movement in the remote key of B flat,
the main key of the work should be specially emphasized. This
impression once clearly conveyed, the harmony, after all, swerves
boldly aside, and in D major there enters the most prominent
theme in the finale.

Ex. 13.

Other themes that are used with a sense of being transitional
material are Ex. 12 (soon taken up with majestic passion by the
whole orchestra) and a combination of it with new figures—

Ex. 14;

foreshadowing the second subject itself.

Ex. 15.

Out of these materials the scheme of exposition and recapitulation
is easy to follow, and soon runs its course. It accordingly lands
us in B major; and now, in what is formally speaking the coda of the
work, comes the real series of events for which all this is a prelude.
The second theme of the slow movement, Ex. 8, enters in B major

adapted to the tempo of the finale, and is brought by both the solo violin and the orchestra through a wide range of key to a climax over which the themes proper to the finale (Exx. 13 and 12) return in full vigour.

Suddenly the music dies away into the minor, and the themes of the first movement reappear slowly and mysteriously (Exx. 1, 4, and 5) in the cadenza, which has become famous as one of the most original dialogues between a solo instrument and an orchestra that have ever been imagined. The device of the 'pizzicato tremolo', which Elgar has invented in this passage, ought henceforth to be a matter of common knowledge in orchestral music. There is nothing like it for filmy harmonious transparency and mystery; and it is one of the simplest things in the world. But we wrong this cadenza if we ascribe its aesthetic value to an orchestral effect. The priceless thing is to find such devices invented in the service of music which enshrines a soul. It is not a sensational effect; and those who have heard of it by reputation and expect to be startled by it will be disappointed. It is simply a common-sense solution of the problem of providing an exquisitely faint harmony that will keep entirely in the background on any notes required. After the cadenza, the introduction to the finale is resumed and leads to a brilliant coda in which Exx. 8, 15, and 13 conclude the work in triumph.

VARIATIONS FOR ORCHESTRA, OP. 35

This delightful work, which first revealed to foreign nations that there was more mastery of orchestration, as well as of form, in British music than they were aware of, has been known, with the

connivance of its composer, as the 'Enigma Variations'. One
part of the enigma is, in a sense, musical, and I confess that I do
not know its answer. The 'Enigma', as the theme is called, is
said to be a counterpoint to a well-known tune which is not alluded
to in the variations. This being so, the 'well-known tune' and the
difficulty of guessing what it is are things that do not belong to
the music as we have it. At all events I find nothing enigmatic in
the composition, and until I do I shall not bother my head with an
enigma which concerns no question of mine. Another part of the
enigma is personal; and, as such, is the private affair of the composer and those friends of his whom it concerns. To them it is
probably no enigma. The variations are 'Dedicated to my friends
pictured within', and the evidently delightful people therein
pictured are indicated by initials and pseudonyms. If there is one
thing that music can clearly illustrate without ceasing to be musical,
it is just this kind of character-drawing that is independent of
narrative and concrete fact. At the same time if I were a police-
man I think I should ask Mr. G. R. S. of variation 11 to produce
his dog-licence; the behaviour of those basses paddling, with the
theme, after a stick thrown into the pond by the violins, and the
subsequent barking of the brass, can hardly be mere coincidence.
Even so, the result is quite as musical as if there were no such
things in nature. None of these externals detracts from the pure
musical beauty and value of a work which has long taken rank as
a permanent addition to the classical repertoire. No amount of
practice wears it thin, and there is many an ambitious composer
of brilliant and revolutionary reputation who ought to be taken by
the scruff of his neck and, orchestrally speaking, washed in its
crystal-clear scoring until he learns the meaning of artistic economy
and mastery.

The theme, with its two contrasted strains in minor and major, is
given in its essentials in the following quotation:

Ex. 1.

The variations, with the partial exception of Var. 10 (Dorabella) and the Romance, Var. 13 (***), are all melodic; that is to say, it is the melody, and not essentially the structure or phrasing, which they reproduce. Where the melody is not recognizable, the composer's object is to give an independent episode, after the manner of Schumann's *Études Symphoniques*. These episodes are placed so as to relieve the melodic variations without breaking the coherence of the whole work.

Var. 1 (C. A. E.) is a beautiful glorification of the theme, which we shall encounter again in the finale. To quote Weber's *Oberon*, 'a gentle ray, a milder beam breaks sweetly on' phrase B of the theme when it is here removed to the softer key of E flat.

Var. 2 (H. D. S.-P.), in quick 3/8 time, begins with a fluttering staccato figure in dialogue with the violins, to which anxious harmonies soon enter wailing in the wind. Then the basses enter with A of the theme. When this is done, the fluttering figures are left behind, soon to vanish into darkness.

Var. 3 (R. B. T.) is a kind of mazurka, in the major mode and in a regular form with repeats. B, suddenly removed to F sharp major, is expanded to a climax from which the basses crawl with grotesque mystery back to the graceful, playful opening.

Var. 4 (W. M. B.), 3/4, in the minor again, storms through the whole theme in a violent temper which the feeble-forcible expostulations of a few frightened wood-winds only exasperate.

Var. 5 (R. P. A.), 12/8 and 4/4, in C minor, takes a gloomy view of A, in the bass with a sombre counterpoint in the violins. The flute runs away with B, which allies itself with a new tripping measure. This, however, does not prevail against the serious outlook, and the variation is dying away sadly, when—

Var. 6, 3/2, C major (Ysobel), who must, in her quiet way, be a perfect hostess, discusses the whole theme in a delightful dialogue, led by a solo viola and shared by all the nicest conversationalists in the orchestra. No tea-cup ever had a more delicate aroma than the last long note of the horn with the viola's last word below it: nor is there any exaggeration in calling the whole episode tone-poetry of an order far too high to be damaged by the lightness of its subject.

Var. 7 (Troyte), with his three drums, is as impossible at afternoon tea as Bernard Shaw's Professor Higgins was in his mother's drawing-room. But Pygmalion is a good fellow for all that.

Var. 8 (W. N.), 6/8, G major, restores peace and comfort with an exquisite epigrammatic neatness and amiability.

Var. 9 (Nimrod), 3/4, E flat, strikes a deeper note. The gay company of the others is not rebuked by it, for no one is hard or silly in this symposium; but the unworldly idealism of this new character is completely at home in its surroundings.

Var. 10 (Dorabella), 3/4, G major, is charming, fluttering, a little plaintive, and so constituted as to float inevitably into the middle of the picture.

Var. 11 (G. R. S.), 2/2, G minor, is the man I have already described as probably the owner of a lively retriever.

Var. 12 (B. G. N.) turns the theme into a melancholy serenade for the 'cellos. It leads to—

Var. 13 (***), Romance, a free episode which is indeed the most romantic thing in the work. The sound of a kettledrum-roll, beaten with side-drum-sticks, and the heaving swell of the violas are suggestive of the sea; and this confirms the rumour that the quotation-marks which the composer puts round the first phrase of the wonderful clarinet solo refer to Mendelssohn's overture, *Calm Sea and Prosperous Voyage*, the main theme of which contains the same familiar figure. To explain this typographical detail, however, is not to explain away the originality and depth of this most impressive passage.

Var. 14 (E. D. U.), the finale, rouses us with the approach of a spirited march. When this has reached the height of its course, there is a sudden dramatic stoppage. The wood-wind ask a question which turns out to be a prominent counterpoint in Var. 1 (C. A. E.). That seraphic and sympathetic being thereupon sails in with all its gentle radiance; and the march (the rhythms of which have accompanied this reappearance) resumes its course and rises to a climax which would be solemn but for its irrepressible tendency to hurry. This tendency increases, while the theme strides over the two-time bars in triple rhythm and the organ begins to boom in the background, until at last the great work rushes in semibreves to its cheerful end.[1] Written at the end of the nineteenth century, it had an immediate success which was no more than the twentieth century will deem a bare acknowledgement of its due. A work of the ripest mastery, it is a glorious beacon to the young composer in the storm and stress of ideas not newer than its own.

OVERTURE, 'COCKAIGNE', OP. 40

British music is emerging from various forms of darkness before dawn; and of these forms perhaps the darkest is that which a now almost too popular psychology calls 'the inferiority complex'. When, at the turn of the century, Elgar expressed his love of London in an overture neither more nor less vulgar than Dickens, the principal impression made on the musical criticism of those

---

[1] I am indebted to the original of Var. 8 for information correcting a rumour that the work was at first planned to end quietly. It had ended abruptly but not quietly, and the present coda was a necessary expansion.

ancient days was one of reverential dread at the audacity of an
English composer who handled the resources of sonata form as
if he had the presumption to understand them. There had been
British symphonic works in sonata form before; but orchestration
had not been our forte, and here was sonata form stated in terms
of consummate orchestration. This was clearly wrong; so clearly
that nobody could say why it was wrong. Hence it followed that
the work must be appallingly clever and complicated.

Even now, nobody can say why it is wrong. I believe some think
it vulgar. Nobody nowadays thinks it complicated. There were
people at the end of last century who thought Albert Chevalier's
songs vulgar; presumably because of their dialect. But vulgarity
in the ordinary (or vulgar) offensive sense lies not in dialects and
not in facts, but in errors of valuation. I cannot find vulgarity
in Elgar's Brass Band as it comes blaring down B flat Street, for
I see no evidence that he intends it to strike a religious note, or
a White Man's Burden note, or any note except the healthy note
of marching in good athletic form on a fine day. The *Cockaigne*
Overture is true to nature, and says its say straightforwardly in
terms of the highest art.

Its first theme, of which I quote only one phrase—

Ex. 1.

has a magnificent Cockney accent in that pause on the high C.
A further sequel anticipates (if my chronology is right) by some
years the vogue of the idiom of the Londoner who strongly affirms
that he does *not* think.

Ex. 2.

After a full orchestral counterstatement of Ex. 1, a new theme,
designated by Elgar's favourite mark, *nobilmente*, sounds a deeper
note.

Ex. 3.
Nobilmente.

Rude little street-boys, each conscious of being born with a Lord
Mayor's Mace up his back-bone, are apt, in later developments,
to whistle it away in irreverent diminution, as the *Lehrbuben* in

C

Meistersinger treat the theme of their masters; but at present its dignity is undisturbed.

There are quiet spaces in London, with room for lovers in sunshine and moonshine; and with these the second subject (in E flat) is concerned.

Ex. 4.

But it is also concerned with the irreverent diminishers of Ex. 3, and it has room for a climax based on Ex. 1. Other themes might well deserve quotation as the overture moves quietly to its development, but I have space only for the appearance of the brass band which, after various warnings in distant sounds, bursts round the corner, while all the bells chronicled in 'Oranges and Lemons' ring at random.

Ex. 5.

This conspicuous event is followed by the quietest and most poetic developments in the whole overture, passages as deep as any in all Elgar's works; and when the recapitulation arrives it is expanded with admirable freedom and resource. The brass band returns in C major; and the noble strains of Ex. 3, supported by the organ, lead to a brilliant abrupt end with Ex. 1.

SYMPHONY IN E FLAT, NO. 2, OP. 63

1 *Allegro vivace e nobilmente.* 2 *Larghetto.* 3 Rondo: *Presto.*
4 *Moderato e maestoso.*

On the fly-leaf of this work stands the following inscription: 'Dedicated to the Memory of His Late Majesty King Edward VII. This Symphony designed early in 1910 to be a loyal tribute, bears its present dedication with the gracious approval of His Majesty the King. March 16th 1911.'

Besides this, the symphony takes from Shelley its motto:

> Rarely, rarely, comest thou,
> Spirit of Delight.

The second figure (*b*) of the main theme—

Ex. 1.

may be taken as representing this motto, for it occurs elsewhere
than in the first movement, and generally with a wistfulness as if
it referred to something no longer, or not yet, present in the
impetuous strength displayed here.

Readers who have followed my essay on Elgar's *Falstaff*
(p. 7) may find it interesting to note how much easier is the
analysis of a work of similar calibre that proceeds on the lines
of classical sonata form. This is not because classical forms are
simpler. On the whole they are more complex than those of
Falstaff. Nor are the forms of *Falstaff* non-classical. The only
conception of form that has any truth in it is that according to which
the form represents the natural growth of the matter so intimately
that, in the last resort, form and matter are interchangeable terms.
But it saves an immense amount of trouble in analysis if the matter
happens to grow into forms which have enough family likeness to
those of many other works of art to have produced a number of
technical terms by which they can be named. Thanks to the very
complexity and richness of the forms of a classical symphony, I am
saved the trouble of trying to identify this or that feature, structural
or emotional, of the present work with the glories and sorrows of
the reign of Edward VII. It is perhaps permissible to say that no
one who has met the composer or studied this symphony can
possibly fail to see that it is animated by no mere official imperialism,
but by a deep glow of personal and affectionate loyalty.

The first movement begins at once with its main theme, containing, as I have said before, in figure (*b*), the musical representa-
tion of its motto. This is the beginning of a long paragraph which
builds into large sequences a number of other themes, from which
I quote three.

Ex. 2.

Ex. 3.

Ex. 4.

As in the Violin Concerto and other large works of Elgar, the
sequential structure and the shortness of the figures built up therein

are apt to produce an analysis like that of the Wagnerian *motiv-*
hunter, according to which the music would appear lamentably
short of breath and still more lamentably long of procedure. As a
matter of fact, Elgar's paragraphs are big and his action is swift.
I have not quoted all the themes of the first group. The tonic,
E flat, stands firm at the outset and the drift towards another key
is sudden and decisive. But when that other key appears it proves
an iridescent mixture of several keys, remote enough for the home
tonic itself to appear foreign in its new surrounding as one of the
chords of the main theme in the second group.

Ex. 5.

The orthodox dominant is more nearly concerned in the
following accessory theme—

Ex. 6.

and various sequences that arise on the materials of Exs. 5 and 4
tend more and more to establish it.

I leave the double climax, at first brilliant and hereafter solemn,
to speak for itself, and I quote only the quiet cadence theme into
which the exposition subsides.

Ex. 7.

From this it passes without perceptible break into the
development, which begins by alternating the expiring strains of
Ex. 7 with a new figure—

Ex. 8.

in a series of remote modulations. These lead to E major, in which
remote key the development takes action by using a combination of
Exs. 8 and 1 as accompaniment to an important new episodic theme.

Ex. 9.

This falls in sequence, descending by semitones in bold dissonance over a persistent E natural, until at last the E gives way and both figures of the first theme (Ex. 1) appear in C major, associated with a new figure.

Ex. 9 a (compare Ex. 5):

The development is chiefly concerned with these materials, alternating with developments of Exs. 4, 2, and 3.

As soon as the quiet episode dies away, the action becomes rapid; and the last stage of the development, in which the figures (a) (b) of Ex. 1 reappear, moves swiftly to a grandiose return prepared for by a solemn summons from the horns and trombones. The recapitulation of both groups is regular, though the handling of the mixed tonalities of the second group has a classical subtlety and freedom.

The coda arises naturally from the expiring of the cadence group (Ex. 7) and, without alluding either to Exs. 8 or 9, proceeds to give Ex. 9 a, augmented to twice its size, pianissimo in the tonic, after which it builds up a quick crescendo on Ex. 3, and ends with an appeal to the Spirit of Delight (Ex. 1, figure (b)).

The slow movement is elegiac, with something of the character of a funeral march. Its first seven bars are an introduction, which I do not quote, on a figure somewhat reminiscent of Ex. 2. It is the main theme—

Ex. 10:

to which this movement chiefly owes its suggestiveness of a funeral march; and that characteristic is perhaps more inherent in the accompaniment than in the melody. (Note the figure (a), common to Exs. 1 and 10. With Elgar such points are significant.)

A modulating transition-theme—

Ex. 11:

leads towards F major, and in a tonal region compounded of that key and of A minor, one of the main themes of the middle section appears.

Ex. 12.

Moving in broad lines and with free rhythm, as if Bruckner had become a master of phrasing, this passes through an agitated sequence on a new figure which I do not quote, to a grand and simple climax fully in F major, with another important theme which completes the exposition.

Ex. 13.

This dies away, and Ex. 11 effects a mournful return to C minor and to the main theme, which is given in full with the addition of a beautiful ruminating counterpoint on an oboe. The whole of the sequel is recapitulated in due order, Exs. 12–13 being given in and around E flat.

The coda arises from a dramatic return to the dominant of C, upon which is heard an appeal to the Spirit of Delight (Ex. 1), alternating with Ex. 11, after which the movement expires in a mournful allusion to the first phrase of its main theme (Ex. 10), which closes into another allusion to the unquoted introductory bars.

The scherzo is, as its title shows, in rondo form. A mystery underlies its playful opening theme.

Ex. 14.

The meaning of the portion marked *x* in this quotation will appear later.

The first episode is in the tonic minor.

Ex. 15.

Considerable development of the figures of the main theme, at first in cross accents and then in combination with a new figure—

Ex. 15 *a*.

follows before the main theme is allowed to return in full. The second episode is in an unorthodox key or tonal region, that of the major supertonic, D.

A wistful introductory figure—

Ex. 16.

is delivered and echoed by several wood-wind instruments, and afterwards worked into paragraphs together with the swinging theme of the episode itself.

Ex. 17.

The second return of the main theme is a quiet affair, and the strings have a tendency to adorn the outline of the group *x* with a halo. This halo becomes gradually clearer until, in the key of E flat, it takes solid shape as the important episodic theme (Ex. 9) with which the development of the first movement had begun. On a long tonic pedal this episode now grows to a mighty cantabile, which eventually passes, via the trombones, into the bass, while the scherzo-theme just contrives to penetrate the mass of tone above. As the mass of tone dies away, another origin of the theme, Ex. 8, becomes audible. It is always an interesting problem in aesthetics how, when a lively movement has mounted on to a sublime pedestal, it can come off it again. Elgar's solution of this dangerous problem is Schumannesque and classical. Without any preaching or tub-thumping, the music resumes the first episode (Ex. 15) quietly, as Schumann's Florestan, or any other nice young undergraduate, might relight his pipe after he had allowed it to go out during an outburst of enthusiasm. As before, steps towards a return to the main theme are taken by a development of Ex. 14, with cross accents; but what is reached is Ex. 15 *a* in a grand climax without the semiquaver figure. When this has died away, the rest of the coda piles itself up in brilliant cross-rhythmed sequences.

The finale seems to be, as the directions for its tempo imply, a comparatively slow movement; but this is rather an illusion of notation, for it is in reality remarkably swift, with an irresistible momentum in the strength of its current. No stronger contrast could be found than that between it and the standard difficulty of the clever composers whose finales and thematic transformations call themselves prestissimo in a vain struggle against the flaccid uniformity of their phrase-lengths.

The finale moves on the lines of a broad sonata form with the following tune as its main theme:

Ex. 18.

A transition theme, starting in the subdominant—

Ex. 19.

leads in massive sequences to a second group consisting of a single new theme in the dominant—

Ex. 20.

closing with a four-bar allusion to Ex. 18. This plunges into a development consisting mainly of a fugue on the figures of Ex. 19 combined with new counterpoint. The tendency of fugues is not to modulate widely. They are arguments rather than actions, or they are actions at law rather than at large. Accordingly the venue of this development remains in the tonal region around D major and B minor, in which latter key the first figure of the main theme (Ex. 18) begins to assert itself obstinately.

A new figure—

Ex. 21.

brings a persuasively pacifying note into the discussion, and soon combines with larger portions of the main theme. Eventually a return to E flat is effected, and the more or less regular recapitulation of all the material builds itself up into a grand climax and leads to a peaceful coda. From the quiet heights into which it recedes, this coda is dominated by the Spirit of Delight (figure (*b*) of Ex. 1 in very slow tempo) and the symphony ends in solemn calm.

CONCERT OVERTURE, 'IN THE SOUTH' (ALASSIO), OP. 50

I have not been to Alassio, and so I cannot talk of Elgar's special sources of inspiration for this brilliant and sunshiny overture. I only hope that, if I ever do go there, I may not find myself in the position of the old lady who said to Turner that she could not see in sunsets anything like his pictorial representations of them; to which, of course, he replied, 'Don't you wish you could?' If she could, she would not have been able to find words for them; and if ever I can see at places like Alassio what Elgar saw as he saw it, I would much rather write a concert overture about it than an analytical programme.

There is still a suspicion of faintness in praising a work for its orchestration, though the time has perhaps passed since nobility was thought to be inherent in clumsy scoring; but, so long as tastes differ as to a composer's style, there is something to be said for calling the listener's attention to a merit which every competent judge must admit to be supreme, not only in its artistic results, but in its practical efficiency. I shall not easily forget my impression when, on first attacking this overture with considerable fear and expectation of its being as difficult as it is brilliant, I found that it simply carried the orchestra away with it and seemed to play itself at the first rehearsal. On inquiry, I found that one single member of the orchestra was not reading it at sight. This exception, of course, accounted for the whole phenomenon, and I am far from claiming that the rehearsal was such as I should willingly accept in lieu of a performance. But I and my students have never had a more impressive demonstration of the enormous efficiency of Elgar's scoring. In brilliance the nearest approach to it in other modern music is the scoring of Richard Strauss; and Elgar and Strauss have in common a panache which is popularly expressed in both the title and the substance of Elgar's *Pomp and Circumstance* Marches, and mystically expressed in the best parts of Strauss's *Heldenleben*. But the scores of Strauss bristle with technical abnormalities, and he drives through his musical traffic like a road-hog, with a mastery that has merely overawed the police

without reforming the rules of the road. Some think that even
Ein Heldenleben is now wearing too thin to reward the labour of
thirty rehearsals for the purpose of securing accuracy where the
composer merely intends effrontery.

To the Straussian panache Elgar adds the enormous sonority
and cogency of a style which is meticulously pure. This is a matter
of fact, and not of taste. Perhaps the word 'meticulous' may be
misleading, and 'classical' might be a better epithet. But I think
'meticulous' is right. Whether you are carried away by Elgar's
style or whether you dislike it, there is no doubt that it is not the
style of a man who is at ease in himself or in Zion. Neither in
poetry nor in music is the atmosphere of *The Dream of Gerontius*
that of a muscular Christian after Charles Kingsley's heart; and
those for whom Kipling's sixth-form imperialism obliterates his
art will not like *Pomp and Circumstance*. But I should be surprised
if the most nervous of reasonable music-lovers could not enjoy *In
the South*. When it appeared in 1904, any approach to mastery
of instrumental form on the part of a British composer was still
considered dangerous. I cannot remember whether *In the South*
had a better reception than the *Cockaigne* Overture; but it is both
a larger and a simpler work, of which the portion normally devoted
to developments is occupied by two detachable episodes. When
Steinbach conducted it at a concert of English music at Cologne
in, I think, 1906, I was surprised to find that he thought it patchy.
That impression probably arose from these episodes, but I am
sure that it is a superficial impression, perhaps intensified by the
comparative orthodoxy and greater concentration of the other
works played on that occasion. In itself, *Alassio* is by no means a
loose-knit work. It has more unity than the *Enigma* Variations,
and far more coherence than Elgar's First Symphony. Classical
overtures, especially when they are preludes to operas, do not pro-
fess to have the concentrated texture of symphonic movements,
and my most beloved overtures of Weber are things of shreds and
patches compared to *Alassio*.

Elgar begins with a group of heroic themes swinging along at
full speed from the outset.

There are more of these than it is necessary to quote, but Ex. 1
shows itself as a counterpoint to all the others. The initial impetus

is strong enough to survive a solemn climax marked by Elgar's favourite direction, *Nobilmente*.

Ex. 3.

After an apparently casual incident in the decline—

Ex. 4.

a pair of gentler themes appears in C minor—

Ex. 5.

Ex. 6.

and leads to a quiet second group, passionately lyrical, in duple time and the extremely unorthodox key of F major.

Ex. 7.

Ex. 8.

Even in the tranquillity of Ex. 8, Ex. 1 intrudes as a counterpoint. Soon Exx. 5 and 6 bring about a gradual revival of energy and carry us into the current of a vigorous development. But this does not last long before we are confronted with a terrifically impressive structure.

Ex. 9.

Ex. 10.

I shall be highly pleased with myself if any Roman bridge or
viaduct, at Alassio or elsewhere, can make an impression on me
that is not mainly dominated by my knowledge of this magnificent
passage with its superbly proportioned repetitions, climax, and
diminuendo. People differ greatly in the extent to which sounds
suggest visual impressions. With me this happens very rarely, but
then very intensely; and Ex. 10 gives me the strongest suggestion
of a horizontal line of roadway immensely high up, with the piers
descending from it into greater and greater depths along a precipi-
tous hill-side.

After the vision has become distant, the progress of development
is resumed with a new bustling theme.

Ex. 11.

Eventually Ex. 1 intervenes, and there is another glimpse of the
bridge or viaduct before Ex. 11 is resumed. The incident quoted
in Ex. 4 becomes important in an impressive diminuendo, typical
of Elgar's most mystic style; and eventually we have what has
become known in a separate arrangement as a piece for small
orchestra, *Canto Popolare* (*In Moonlight*). As a separate piece it is
a very pretty thing, but in its context in this Overture it is as gravely
and romantically beautiful as music can be.

Ex. 12.
Viola solo.

Quiet and slow reminiscences of Ex. 1 intervene contrapuntally, and
there are warnings of a revival of energy in allusions to Exx. 4 and 5.

The *Canto Popolare* dies away, and in the original key and tempo Ex. 1 returns pianissimo, but with a rapid crescendo which soon brings us into the full swing of a regular recapitulation of everything from Exx. 1 to 8: the F major group from 6 to 7 being, of course, now in the home tonic. From the quiet end of this recapitulation arises Ex. 3, a fourth lower and in the tenderest pianissimo. It swells out and leads to fresh developments of the livelier themes in a noble coda which is one of the best of all Elgar's perorations, its rhetoric entirely unspoilt by tub-thumping, and leaving us with a magnificent impression of punctuality in its end.

INTRODUCTION AND ALLEGRO FOR STRINGS
(QUARTET AND ORCHESTRA), OP. 47

Comparisons of this important work with the concerto grosso of the early eighteenth century are misleading. In its form and texture there is neither the antiquity of Wardour Streete Englisshe nor that of the genuine furniture that may be bought in that street by those who know. It is a piece of modern music, modern in the lasting sense of the term. That is to say, its date, 1905, is no more identifiable in 1937 than it will be in 2005. The kind of concerto form which it embodies is in line with Beethoven and Brahms, and definitely out of line with Handel and Bach. The sound of the strings, in both solo and tutti, will remind us of the older masters, simply because the Concerti Grossi of Handel and his predecessors and the third Brandenburg Concerto of Bach are the only classical works for string orchestra that we ever hear, with the solitary exception of Mozart's toy masterpiece, *Eine Kleine Nachtmusik*. But if it had ever occurred to Beethoven or Brahms to experiment with the problem of concerto form for an orchestra of strings alone, they would have produced something with the essential features of the present work. It is highly probable that, like Elgar, they would have treated the contrast between string quartet and string tutti as rather a matter of fine shades than of the intense dramatic opposition of solo and orchestra that inspired them when the orchestra was full. Also the fitness of the occasion for fugue-writing would not have escaped their notice, nor would they have been slow to take advantage of it.

In the present work, as in others, Elgar's form is his own; and doubtless Beethoven and Brahms would each have achieved a different and unique solution of its special problem. A long classical orchestral ritornello has another function besides that of giving scope to the full orchestra. It presents the main features of the movement in an introductory form. This introduction naturally has a processional character when the ritornello is long; and only something highly dramatic can be justified in curtailing it. Hence nothing could be more appropriate than that, instead of the formal ritornello, the present work should have a grand introduction in which the themes appear at first as fragments in a highly dramatic dialogue between orchestra and quartet; the united forces propounding a sternly majestic question—

to which the quartet adds another in wistful tones—

After the dialogue has made some progress with the discussion the viola is allowed to give full lyric form to a new melody in E flat—

which the quartet and orchestra take up with quiet enthusiasm. Ex. 1 intervenes again dramatically, bringing back the key of G minor. The lyric melody pathetically accepts the decision; but its dying fall, after a long pause, resolves in the cheerful and active daylight with which the allegro now begins.

Nobody could have foreseen what the functions of these themes are now to be. Ex. 2, with its typically Elgaresque quick dactylic figure, becomes the main theme. A new three-bar theme, stated in a lower octave by the quartet and answered by the tutti—

executes a broadly designed transition to the dominant, in which key the second group begins in triumph. The *a-priori* theorist expects it to consist of an enlargement of the lyric melody, Ex. 3. It proves, on the contrary, to consist of a grand tutti on Ex. 1, in terms of the utmost confidence and power, worked out in a brilliant paragraph, the close of which is reached through an allusion to Ex. 4. Suddenly, as the figure of Ex. 1 reverberates above, through and below the last chords, the beginning of the

lyric melody is faintly heard in a tremulous unison of the muted
string quartet—a moment of romantic power worthy to be set by
the Romanza in the *Enigma* Variations. A lively fugue in G minor
has the function of the development-portion of the work. It exercises this function the more efficiently by being completely independent of previous themes. In all genuine concerto styles the
exposition itself is compelled by circumstances to have many
features more typical of development than of exposition; and thus
only by means of episodic matter can the development-portion
maintain a character of its own.

Here is the new fugue-subject—

Ex. 5.

The key-changes of fugues are necessarily drifting rather than
sharply contrasted. In as far as a fugue can be dramatic it is a
debate; and dramatic action will probably stop a debate alto-
gether. Hence Elgar leaves us to discover only when this debate
has reached its climax that we have been at home in the tonic all
the time. (No two works could be less like each other than this
allegro and the finale of Beethoven's Sonata, op. 101, but you will
find exactly the same phenomenon there, as a result of the same
insight into the nature of music.) As the fugue dies away, allusions
to the transition theme (Ex. 4) indicate that the most episodic of
developments can be organically connected with the exposition so
long as there is a B in Both.

A full and regular recapitulation brings symmetry into the
design; but the symmetry extends beyond the allegro and includes
the Introduction; for the lyric melody, Ex. 3, is now neither a far-
off echo nor a gentle strain with a dying fall for the ear of Duke
Orsino, but a solemn triumphal march of full Elgarian pomp.

Throughout the whole work the instrumentation has all Elgar's
subtlety and consummate mastery, shown more obviously by the
limited means here available, though not more perfectly than in
works for full orchestra.

VAUGHAN WILLIAMS

CONCERTO ACCADEMICO, IN D MINOR, FOR VIOLIN AND STRING ORCHESTRA

1 Allegro pesante. 2 Adagio. 3 Presto.

Why *Accademico*? This work is certainly written in no ancient style. Perhaps it is 'academic' in the sense that it is strictly consistent in its own rules; and perhaps the composer wishes to indicate that in his opinion these rules are by this time so well established that they ought to be taught in schools. If such an opinion is correct, I fear that the University of Edinburgh will remain behind the times as long as I am there. It is one thing, and a thing both feasible and necessary, to bring students to understand and enjoy music that would be completely unintelligible to any composer of sixty years ago; it is quite another matter to set about devising exercises in its grammar to students who find the elements of the classical grammar difficult.

If to be academic is to be of crystalline clearness and symmetry, this work is as academic as Mozart or Bach or any classical master, whether he was, like Mozart, abreast of his time, or, like Bach, ninety years behind it and ahead of any assignable future time. Another quality that may be put down to the credit of academic art is consistency of style. Everybody knows that Vaughan Williams is intensely English, that he is an enthusiastic and expert collector of English folk-songs, and that he has learnt much from modern French music in general and from Ravel in particular. But though it may amuse a certain kind of expert to trace these origins in his music, it is quite unnecessary for the intelligent enjoyment of it. He has made a style of his own out of whatever interests him, and no composer is less liable to fall into reminiscences of other music.

So let us listen to this concerto without further prejudice as to what is or is not academic (such as Consecutive Fifths, the Ottava Battuta, the False Relation of the Tritone, and other progressions condemned as licentious by the Great Masters of the Golden Rockstro), and let us also not inquire further into such private affairs as the origins of the composer's ideas. Whatever the origin, the results are true to them, for the results are original. This is no pun, but a statement of fact. The original artist is, as Swift pointed out in *The Battle of the Books*, not the spider whose unpleasant and glutinous web is merely his own unpleasant inside turned outwards, but the bee whose honey is skilfully wrought from its source in the flowers.

The *Concerto Accademico* begins with a spirited ritornello theme—

in which the solo violin plays with the orchestra, emerging in a high fifth here and there. Soon the solo makes its official entry with a new theme derived by diminution from the fourth bar (*a*) of the main theme.

After a short cadenza Ex. 1 is resumed. With sudden change of key a new theme enters, also derived from (*a*)—

and lending itself to decoration by the figure of Ex. 1. An incident in cross-rhythm adds a note of romantic mystery to the Bach-like, imperturbable amble of the whole.

Then the figures of Ex. 1 and 2 are developed *seriatim* and combined in new sequences, over which a new theme emerges as a counterpoint in one part after another.

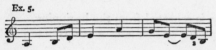

This development leads to a recapitulation of the previous themes in the tonic, followed by a coda in which Ex. 4 plays its part.

The slow movement is another Bach-like scheme, in which a

solo violoncello joins with the solo violin. The main theme, in a Dorian G minor—

Ex. 6.

alternates with a 'soft Lydian air' (Ionian or Aeolian, as you may prefer)—

Ex. 7.

which eventually modulates widely in combination with Ex. 5, and finally settles in the original Dorian mode.

The finale is a jig, of which the main theme borrows features from a theme in the opera *Hugh the Drover*.

Ex. 8.

Another tune in triple time combines with this duple jig-measure.

Ex. 9.

In a kind of Aeolian-Mixolydian dominant key a new jig-theme forms the second element in a terse binary scheme.

Ex. 10.

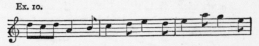

Above it a counterpoint is added.

Ex. 11.

The exposition is repeated from the beginning.

The development section adds a new counterpoint—

Ex. 12.

which is afterwards used to weld the recapitulation to the coda, in which three themes are combined (Exs. 9, 11, 12); the Dorian mode giving place to D major, in which key the concerto comes to the quietest and most poetically fantastic and convincing end imaginable.

PASTORAL SYMPHONY

1 *Molto moderato.* 2 *Lento moderato.* 3 *Moderato pesante.*
4 *Lento, leading to* 5 *Moderato maestoso.*

In his Pastoral Symphony Vaughan Williams has set his imagination at work on lines which at no point traverse the ground covered by Beethoven. The very title of Beethoven's first movement shows that Beethoven is a town-dweller who is glad of a holiday in the country; and the other scenes, by the brook, at the country-dance, and during and after the thunder-storm, are all conceived as interesting to the visitor who has left town for the sake of the experience. The experience is deep and poetic; but Beethoven never thought of describing any of his compositions as a 'town' sonata or symphony. One does not describe what has never been conceived otherwise. Now Vaughan Williams's Pastoral Symphony is born and bred in the English countryside as thoroughly as the paintings of Constable. If he had not given us his London Symphony we should have no artistic evidence that this composer had ever thought of town in his life. But whether in town or in the country, this music is contemplative in a way that was not possible a century ago. Beethoven's nature-worship has much in common with Wordsworth's; but since that time pantheism and mysticism have gone a long way further towards Nirvana.

Beethoven's touch, in his Pastoral Symphony, is so light that, as with Mozart *passim*, the listener forgets the power. In Vaughan Williams's Pastoral Symphony the listener cannot miss the sense of power behind all this massive quietness; it is as manifest in the music as in a bright sky with towering, sunlit, cumulus clouds—and as little likely to rouse us to action. Across this landscape of saturated colours there float the sounds of melodies older than any folk-song. These melodies are harmonized on the plan first reduced to formula by Debussy: whatever chord the melody begins with is treated as a mere sensation, and the chord follows the

melody up and down the scale, instead of dissolving into threads
of independent melodic line. But Vaughan Williams adds to this
principle another, which is that two or even three melodic threads
may run simultaneously, each loaded with its own chord, utterly
regardless of how their chords collide. The collisions will not
offend the naïve listener if they occur only between sounds on
planes of tone so different that they do not blend. As applied to
classical counterpoint this principle is as old as Bach; but the
systematic application of it to the anti-contrapuntal method of
Debussy is new. Bi-planar or tri-planar harmony is what the
theorists call it; and it is both more schematic and more free in
this work than in most of the examples that have been discussed
and quoted during the last twenty years. Earlier examples have
generally had one of the parts standing comparatively still, like an
ornamented organ-point; but such a passage as Ex. 3 shows rigid
chords moving quite freely in three planes of harmony.

The symphony begins with a soft, waving figure below which
a theme appears in the bass:

Ex. 1.

The harp supplies a full chord to each note. A solo violin, imitated
by an oboe, answers with another figure.

Ex. 2.

The first theme is then given in imitation between treble and bass.
I quote in order to show the 'tri-planar' harmony.

Ex. 3.

Other themes, some less serene, follow; of which it will suffice to quote two: the one a mysterious pair of chords, to which a cor anglais adds a plaintive question—

Ex. 4.

&c.

and the other a salient example of the pentatonic melodies with which the whole symphony abounds.

Ex. 5.

These and similar materials are worked up quietly and combined, coming at last to a climax from which the movement descends to a pianissimo end on the first notes of Ex. 1.

The second movement is built from two pentatonic melodies—

Ex. 6.

and—

Ex. 7.

both of which stand out against the dark background of a chord of F minor.

Later on a trumpet is heard, playing in the natural harmonic series of E flat. This natural series, which is that of the overtones of a pipe, extends of course *ad infinitum*, but before it has reached its tenth note it has already included one note which has never been absorbed in the classical system of harmony.

Ex. 8

1 2 3 4 5 6 7 8 9 10

The seventh note of this series is flatter than any B flat recognizable either in mathematically pure classical harmony or in the mechanical average embodied in our tempered scale. But to call it unnatural would be like calling a Frenchman a foreigner in Paris because he did not speak English.

The ninth note of the natural series is, again, not the same as the corresponding tempered note; but its exact intonation is thoroughly realized in the classical system, as Helmholtz found when he tested Joachim's intonation on the violin. Obviously the pianoforte, which is obliged to make the interval from C to D equal to that from D to E cannot distinguish the ratio 8 : 9 from the ratio 9 : 10. A trumpet, however, that renounces the use of modern valves and relies entirely on lip-pressure, is not only able to distinguish these ratios and to add to them the musically unknown ratio 7 : 8, but it cannot possibly get them wrong. Accordingly in this passage the trumpet declaims in free rhythm on these natural sounds. This is the central feature of the movement. At the end a natural horn in F repeats this trumpet-passage in combination with Ex. 6.

In the scherzo a rustic human element seems present, rather at work than at play. (The composer tells me that the element is not human: the music was sketched for a ballet of oafs and fairies.)

Ex. 9.

This alternates with another theme in livelier time.

Ex. 10.

A warbling figure, given out by the flute, follows and combines with these. Later a spirited tune in a Mixolydian scale dances its way in the brass and the full orchestra, constituting the trio of the scherzo.

Ex. 11.

The scherzo returns, rescored; and likewise, for a few lines, the theme of the trio. Patient beasts of burden are manifest as well as human (or oafish) labourers. But the movement unexpectedly subsides in a mysterious fugue—

Ex. 12.

which explains itself by combining first with a variant of the (unquoted) warbling theme, and then with it and Ex. 10. And so the gnats (or the fairies) have it all their own way.

The finale is a slow movement. It begins with a deep soft roll of the drum, over which a distant human voice (or, if necessary, a clarinet) sings a wordless rhapsody in a pentatonic scale.

Then, after some introductory bars, the following tune is announced:

Ex. 13.

An agitated utterance of the cor anglais, taken up by the solo violin, gives rise eventually to one of the serenest passages in the whole work. It is the shape towards which the phrases of the distant voice were tending at the outset.

Ex. 14.

The solo violin intervenes passionately, and leads to a climax in which all the strings declaim the vocal opening. They die away into a figure of accompaniment below which Ex. 13 returns in all its solemnity. Eventually, the symphony ends with the distant voice no longer over a drum-roll, but under a high note sustained like the clear sky.

OVERTURE TO 'THE WASPS'

The plays of Aristophanes give the composer abundant opportunities for music; and Vaughan Williams has made brilliant use of those afforded by *The Wasps*. Besides the choruses, which are restricted and inspired by the elaborate precision of Greek metrical forms, there is material in the incidental music for an effective orchestral suite. Of this the overture, to be performed on the present occasion, is the largest and most developed movement. I have not at hand the means of assigning its various themes to precise functions in the Aristophanic drama, nor is this aspect a matter of Wagnerian importance. The Athenians, according to the play, were going through a phase of litigious mania, for which the demagogue Cleon was largely to blame. Law-suits have bereft poor old Philocleon of whatever wits he once had, and he makes his entry up through the chimney, explaining that he is the smoke. His son Bdelycleon can keep him quiet only by occupying him with the trial of a dog, with counsel for prosecution and defence, pathetic exhibition of the wailing about-to-be dispossessed or orphaned puppies, &c., all complete. The chorus, appropriate to the Athenian temper, is a chorus of wasps.

The overture accordingly presents a compendium of Aristophanic matters, of which the main sentiment is that the Athenians are good-natured healthy enough people, if only they would not allow demagogues to lead them by the nose. Accordingly, apart from the normal Gregorian tones of a wasps' nest, the music consists of a brilliant scheme of tunes galore, in the style of folk-songs, diatonic by nature, but occasionally inveigled by Cleon into a whole-toned scale. I am not interested to know which, if any, of these tunes are actual folk-melodies. Vaughan Williams ranks with Marjorie Kennedy-Fraser among the supreme discoverers and recorders of genuine folk-music; but he can invent better tunes than any that will ever be discovered by research. And if he himself were to tell me that there were pantomimic topical allusions to Aristophanes in the original folk-poems of his tunes, I fear I should be strongly tempted to extemporize additions to such details until my whole analysis became a 'leg-pull'. The listener may be further reassured on another point. The music owes nothing to researches for ancient Greek musical fragments; its archaisms are the latest (or nearly the latest) modernisms of a lover of British folk-music, and it has no tendency to base 'We won't go home till morning' on the supertonic of a minor key, and sing it in five-eight time, thus—

as is the way of composers too learned in ancient Greek music.[1] Here, then, are the main themes of this overture. First a rowdy couple of dance-measures, with a tendency to combine in primitive counterpoint.

Ex. 1.

[1] This diatribe is emphatically not directed against the wonderful ancient Greek melody so beautifully used in Ethel Smyth's *The Prison*. I will not stir up wasps' nests by explaining what it is directed against.

Ex. 2.

Lastly, a gentle, broad melody first stated by itself in E flat and, in the final stage of the movement, combined as follows with Ex. 1.

Ex. 3.

ARTHUR SOMERVELL

VIOLIN CONCERTO IN G MINOR

1 *Allegro moderato.* 2 *Adagio.* 3 *Allegro giocoso.*

There will never be too many violin concertos in the world. They are immensely difficult to write, even on post-classical or experimental lines; and while violinists clamour for additions to their repertoire, they find more difficulty in learning new concertos than in keeping their classical repertoire up to the demands of their engagements. Accordingly a new concerto will have a better chance if its design is a light post-classical framework for the display of the violin than if it is either on full-sized classical lines or experimental in the latest phases of revolution. Nevertheless, some living composers are so fond of music that the full-sized classical form of concerto still gives them a greater stimulus to musical invention than any other; and so Sir Edward Elgar designed his Violin Concerto with a broad opening tutti and a full exploitation of the consequences thereof. And now Sir Arthur Somervell does likewise. The two works resemble the classics no more than they resemble each other. They agree with the classics and with each other in being individuals, in owing their form to their matter, and (a third way of saying the same thing) in being the work of masters who know their own minds and are not diverted from saying what they mean by any consideration as to whether 'one can do this nowadays'.

The Somervell Violin Concerto is easy to follow, and is in fact so much less complex than the Elgar that the comparison between the two cannot possibly illuminate either of them. Unfortunately the comparison is quite certain to be made by most people who know that both works are violin concertos and both are by contemporary Englishmen. Accordingly, let the possibility of comparison here be mentioned as a subject hereafter under taboo. The Elgar Concerto is obviously the more difficult to understand and to play. The Somervell Concerto will, like most of its author's works, attract the listener at once, and will not present him with anything evidently difficult to understand. The wise listener will, nevertheless, refrain from concluding that what he appreciates on a first hearing comprises the whole work in all its dimensions and implications; nor will he be worried by that most destructive of prejudices, the belief that what pleases immediately must always be wrong somehow. This belief has never been shared by great masters. They know that bad works may be 'best sellers'; but they have no conviction that good works may not; and their own criteria are far too humdrum to impress as profound criticism. The highest praise ever given by one great composer to another was Haydn's oft-quoted assertion to Leopold Mozart; but usually only the unimportant half of it is quoted. 'I assure you', said Haydn, 'that your son is the greatest musician I have ever seen or heard of.' Very generous and superlative, but not so pregnant as the continuation: 'he has taste and the most thorough knowledge of composition'.

And now let us all devote what taste and knowledge of composition we possess to the enjoyment of a violin concerto by a composer who has abundance of melodious and rhythmic invention, and whose technical resources are all devoted to making his music clear. This end he attains so thoroughly that probably few listeners will realize how free his rhythms are, and how impossible it is to predict what turn the end of a phrase will take. I purposely quote the themes only as far as the first square section: the continuations are always inevitable when we have heard them, but never predictable. The harmonic style is in keeping with the themes and rhythms; the treatment of the minor mode is tinged with the Doric and Aeolian of English and kindred folk-song, while the key-system of the whole work is by no means tied down to classical precedent.

The opening tutti begins with the following main theme—

Ex. 1.

The figure (a) of the first bar is used in several other themes, as later quotations will show. In the rhythm ♪ ♪♪ ♪ | ♩ it pervades the next theme (unquoted), which makes a deliberate symphonic transition to the complementary key (B flat) in which the second group of themes is to be cast. The procedure is that of Joachim's Hungarian Concerto, a modification of Beethoven's in his C minor Concerto, but less symphonic than either. Beethoven's C minor tutti was so thoroughly symphonic that when his second group began in its complementary key Beethoven found himself compelled to shift it back to the tonic before the pianoforte could enter at all; and then the pianoforte had no chance of diverging from a strict recapitulation of the tutti up to that shifting point. Joachim found it possible to let his second group die away before the orchestra had gone far into it; and so his solo arose out of it quietly but dramatically, and there was no difficulty in continuing with freedom throughout. Somervell's tutti has contrived, somehow, to keep its processional and preludial aspect throughout in spite of its apparently symphonic form. The orchestra gives out the two main themes of the second group. Of these the first is a fine example of a long and close-knit musical sentence. I am strongly tempted to quote the whole 18 bars (closing into a 19th as first of the next theme), but the listener may learn more by finding out for himself what comes of the simple-seeming first 4-bar clause.

Ex. 2.

As the melody approaches its close it makes use of figure (a) in smooth rhythm. That figure then takes an entirely different form in the energetic next theme.

Ex. 3.

The above three quotations show that this opening tutti has at

all events this difference from its classical models, that its material
shows three radically different time-measures instead of only one.
There is, nevertheless, a common denominator implied, however it
may yield here and there to rubato. The half-bar of Ex. 1 is the
same size as that of Ex. 2, and as one-third of the bar of Ex. 3.

The orchestra disposes of Ex. 3 in 18 bars, which die away in
evident anticipation of something dramatic. And the solo violin
enters with a solemn meditation in recitative, alluding to figure (a),
and punctuated by pizzicato chords which descend in chromatic
steps from D (the dominant) to the tonic G. The pizzicato chords
settle into a swinging accompaniment to Ex. 1, and the solo violin
proceeds to translate the whole opening tutti into its own language.
But it cannot confine itself to the lines laid down by the orchestra;
it must have a new transition theme, though (a) is still latent.

This leads through one or two new incidents to a regular solo
version of the whole second group (Exx. 2 and 3); to which the
violin adds a serene closing-theme made of figure (a).

A horn repeats this while the solo adorns it with arpeggios. Then
the orchestra intervenes and starts the development in B flat minor.
There is no trace of the classical procedure which is to reproduce,
with or without some new modulation, a substantial portion of the
opening tutti; the orchestra and violin plunge at once into a
discursive development of figure (a) in dialogue and in various
forms new and old, seldom giving more than the first $3\frac{1}{2}$ bars of the
theme as in Ex. 1, but producing several contrasted episodes from
it. Eventually the second group (Ex. 2) intervenes in C major and
moves towards E minor. The solo violin alludes to its opening
cadenza, and the orchestra, apropos of figure (b), enters with a
short crescendo that lands unexpectedly in the tonic major, G.

Hereupon the recapitulation begins, with a triumphant transla-
tion of Ex. 1 into the major mode. The solo violin diverts the
continuation to its own purposes and leads to Ex. 4 in E minor, from
which point the recapitulation becomes exact. The end of Ex. 5

leads to the cadenza. This, though on different lines from those
of the first entry of the solo, somewhat recalls that entry by its
ruminative recitative style and its development of figure (*a*).
During its course the muted strings of the orchestra enter with an
augmentation of Ex. 2, while the solo violin breaks into arpeggios.
The cadenza, however, extends beyond this incident and leads
eventually to a serene coda devoted to Ex. 1 in the major mode.
But at last the tone changes and the theme returns to its original
heroic mood, in which the movement ends.

The slow movement (in E flat) begins with a 4-bar phrase for
low-pitched wind, anticipating and closing into the main theme.
This is given out by the solo violin in a big paragraph with subtle
rhythm, involving in two places a two-beat bar of two beats instead
of three. I give the first six bars, which overlap with the longer
continuation initiated by the entry of the horn.

At the end of the theme a transition-passage leads to a middle
section in the bright key of G major. Its main theme begins in
dominant harmony, thus—

and is continued with an allied theme, also hovering on a half-
close—

which is used separately later on.

The return to the main key and theme is effected in twice two
bars of such masterly poetic power that I must quote them. They
arise out of the tonic chord on which the solo violin has at last
succeeded in resolving the persistent dominant of its themes.
And so the main theme returns, as it were, in mid-stride.

The recapitulation is terse, and on to it is grafted a peaceful coda beginning with Ex. 7, alluding, in cadence, to Ex. 6, and ending with a tonic pedal below an expanded version of the procedure shown in Ex. 9.

The finale is a joyous rondo on lines differing from classical precedent in certain matters of key-relation which need not worry the listener. The quotation of its main themes is all that is needed.

Rondo theme.

The second strain of this theme is on a contrasted figure. There is also a new transition theme arising out of the close, and leading to—

First Episode, or Second Group.

Starting in the orthodox dominant, this soon goes to remoter regions, such as F major, a thoroughly unorthodox key, from which, however, the return to G (and to Ex. 11) is effected with insolent ease, the orchestra seeming to stretch itself in a slow yawn while the solo violin blows smoke-rings.

Second Episode.

Ex. 12.

The supertonic, A minor, is a key which, though closely related to the tonic, is never chosen by classical composers for cardinal features of form. The present unorthodoxy is partly a natural result of the previous unorthodoxy of F major, and for the rest it forms the right base of operations for the subsequent adventures that take us through various other keys and surprise us with incidents like the tutti outburst of Ex. 11, in B major. This outburst eventually shortens the normal course of the finale considerably, for when next the main theme (Ex. 10) returns (on a trumpet) there is no need for another explicit recapitulation of the whole first episode (Ex. 11) in the tonic, but it can be dealt with allusively together with all the other themes, including the unquoted transition theme, in a spacious perorative coda.

'NORMANDY': SYMPHONIC VARIATIONS FOR

PIANOFORTE WITH ORCHESTRA

The title of this work refers to its theme, a folk-song sung at the present day by the peasants of Varangeville. The notion of 'symphonic variations' may perhaps also indicate something a little more definite than the mere general importance of the orchestra in their design: certainly it means more than Schumann meant by *Études Symphoniques*. Sir Hubert Parry's Symphonic Variations are strict variations on a short theme, but grouped in four great sections in tempi corresponding suggestively to the first movement, slow movement, scherzo, and finale of a symphony.

Sir Arthur Somervell's variations are, after the first two formal counterstatements of his 'Norman' theme, free fantasias which cannot possibly be numbered off into single variations. The theme, for that matter, is not a closed melody but rather a thing that returns into itself. But these free fantasias have a very obvious resemblance to the four movements of a symphony; though on this view we must regard the three opening statements of the theme, with the following cadenza and allegro, as an introduction; beginning the main movement at the alla breve time, including its important 3/2 section as a middle part, and calling the later group of variations in 4/4 time either a return to the introduction or the first part of the slow movement. All these questions, however, are of less importance than the natural flow and inexhaustible variety of the whole work, which (in times when the motto of musical fashion is *omne absurdum pro magnifico*) are perhaps not so justly appreciated as the opposite qualities would be revered. At present, when a living composer says anything which can readily be understood, there is a real danger that the arbiters of musical fashion will assume first that they have understood all that he has said, and secondly that he has said nothing. Neither progress nor permanence in the fine arts has ever been secured by arbiters of fashion: it is even doubtful whether they have been hindered by them. When a work of art says a great deal, even the most favourable fashions can popularize only a fraction of its meaning. And, as Ruskin pointed out in one of his clearest and most accurate passages, it is really the loose and obscure writer that is least misunderstood: the clear and accurate writer is always taken up in mid-sentence by the careless reader who thinks he agrees with him.

We have here to deal with a clear and spontaneous work of art, so highly organized that its form is free, and so full of point that its clearness does not exhaust its meaning at a single hearing.

After a short and solemnly dramatic introduction, into which the figures of the theme are introduced by the brass instruments intervening softly in a remote key, the pianoforte states the theme in full, each of the two strophes being repeated by the orchestra.

Ex. 1.

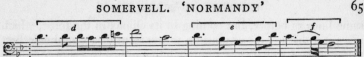

The oboe then takes up the theme, which thereafter bursts out in
the full orchestra, coming at last to a pause which gives occasion
for a cadenza for the pianoforte. Then, in a quick flowing tempo
(allegro), the pianoforte begins a free development from figure (*d*)
of Ex. 1, and continues, in dialogue with the orchestra, by an
impassioned discussion of the three notes comprised in figure (*b*)—
the most important and variously treated figure in the work. In
spite of the interest of this whole passage it does not advance
beyond an introductory manner; the slow tempo returns, with the
mood of the original theme; and the figure (*e*), from its close,
droops away in dreamy modulations; when suddenly a new movement (molto allegro in 2/2 time) starts with a vigorous awakening.

Ex. 2.

Ex. 2 gives its introductory start, showing figure (*b*). The main
new theme, beginning on the tonic, is only harmonically connected
with 'Normandy', but when it shifts its key to B flat the orchestra
surges up with figure (*d*), and then, in D minor, gets into dialogue
with the pianoforte on a new version of (*b*). At the climax there is
a pause, and with a change to 3/2 time the pianoforte, imitated by
various single instruments, works out a sustained and melodious
new development of (*b*).

Ex. 3.

The orchestra interpolates a sentence which puts figure (*d*) into
a similar new light. The pianoforte then resumes its sustained
treatment of (*b*) with a shifted accent and a more flowing accompaniment. Soon the inner parts of the orchestra get to work on
the theme of the molto allegro. The hint is not taken at once;
but eventually, after very remote modulations, the pianoforte asks
suggestive questions, and the horn gives impressive warnings
(figure (*a*), across the 3/2 time). The main theme of the molto
allegro then swings back in such a way that the precise moment of
the change back to 2/2 time is imperceptible. It continues on the

same lines as before, but coming to its climax in the tonic, which
gives it a distinct air of allusion to the form of a symphonic first
movement. Its final close plunges into a return to a slower tempo,
exactly half its pace, and slightly suggestive of the mood of the
opening. What follows is in the manner of a sustained variation
of 'Normandy', chiefly in terms of figure (c). The pianoforte takes
it up serenely with a sudden change to the major mode; and this
change is followed up with increasingly intense calm and happi-
ness. Here for the first time some development is made of the
last figure (f) of the theme. Then the note deepens, as the pianoforte recalls the rhythmic figure of (a) (which has been absent for
some time); and with a change of time a new section begins, which
that figure pervades in great solemnity, with masses of deep
harmony in the brass.

Ex. 4. *Adagio.*

This is worked up with great breadth and swing twice to a solemn
climax and a not less solemn quiet close. When it has died away
the drum turns the rhythmic figure of (a) into a lively introduction
to what may fitly be called a scherzo; of which the main theme is
as follows:

Ex. 5.

It alternates with a trio in which still more of the figures of 'Normandy' are neatly embodied, while the drum maintains the rhythm
of Ex. 5.

Ex. 6.

Modulating widely, this trio leads back to Ex. 5 in a new key, from
which it easily swings back, not to its starting-point, E minor, but
to its second key, G major, and thus rushes straight on into the
finale. This begins in a very original way, with a series of wide

curling arpeggios ending in violent chords on the fourth beat of a 4/4 bar. This explosive utterance conceals a ground bass—

Ex. 7.

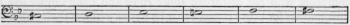

on which the first part of the finale proceeds. The eleven variations on this ground show great variety in their unity; with the fifth there is a change to triple time, to say nothing of the happy entrance of the major mode for this one variation; at the ninth the 4/4 time returns, and the eleventh is a fierce climax. Meantime the figures of 'Normandy' have been very happily interwoven at various points above the ground-bass, so that when the fury of the climax is spent nothing can be more natural than that the tune itself should, especially in its second part with figure (c), swing lustily in and stride from key to key with growing zest until the whole orchestra brings the work to a triumphant end.

WILLIAM WALTON

VIOLA CONCERTO

1 *Andante comodo.* 2 *Vivo, con moto preciso.* 3 *Allegro moderato.*

The style of this work is modern in so far as it could hardly have achieved its present consistency before 1920 (the actual date is 1929); but it does not consist of negatives. Hence it will arouse the anger of many progressive critics and composers in these days of compulsory liberty. Walton's music has tonality, form, melody, themes, and counterpoint. The counterpoint, and hence the harmony, are not always classical. Classical counterpoint is harmony stated in terms of a combination of melodies: classical harmony, when correctly translated from whatever instrumental conditions may have disguised it, is the result of good classical counterpoint where the inner melodic lines are not meant to attract attention. Modern counterpoint tends actually to avoid classical harmony. It prefers that the simultaneous melodies should collide rather than combine; nor does it try to explain away the collisions.

It wishes the simultaneous melodies to be heard; and if they harmonize classically the combination will not assert itself as such. Hence modern counterpoint is no longer a technical matter at all; its new hypothesis has annihilated it as a discipline. But this very fact has thrown new responsibilities on the composer's imagination. A technical discipline becomes a set of habits which, like civilization itself, saves the artist from treating each everyday matter as a new and separate fundamental problem. The rule-of-thumb contrapuntist need not trouble to imagine the sound of his combination; his rules and habits assure him that it cannot sound wrong. The composer who has discarded those rules and habits must use his imagination for every passage that he writes without their guidance. It is by no means true that mere haphazard will suit his purpose. Nor, on the other hand, is it true that any great classical master used rules as a substitute for his imagination. One of the first essentials of creative art is the habit of imagining the most familiar things as vividly as the most surprising. The most revolutionary art and the most conservative will, if they are both to live, have this in common, that the artist's imagination shall have penetrated every part of his work. To an experienced musician every score, primitive, classical, or futurist, will almost at a glance reveal the general question whether the composer can or cannot use his imagination. About details I would not be so sure. To the experienced musician Berlioz has no more business to exist than the giraffe; 'there ain't no such animal'.

Walton is no Berlioz; a glance at his score will suffice to show an art that has been learnt as peacefully as any form of scholarship. And it is possible to read the first twelve bars of this Viola Concerto carefully without finding anything irreconcilable to an academic style in the 'nineties. After the twelfth bar the range of style expands. But let us note that it thereby differs from the many other modern styles which contract. Walton's style is not sentimental; but neither is it anti-romantic.

Similarly, it is neither theatrical nor sensational; and its forms do not at first seem to have more than a slight external resemblance to sonata forms. Yet it has essential qualities of sonata style in its ways of getting from one theme to another and in its capacity to give dramatic meaning to the establishing of a new key. Walton's dramatic power has asserted itself in oratorio; but its unobtrusive presence in this thoughtful piece of purely instrumental music is more significant than any success in an oratorio on the subject of Belshazzar's feast. The sceptical critic can always argue that an oratorio, especially on such a subject, can hardly go wrong unless the librettist's intellect is subnormal. But when a composer can write an effective concerto for viola (an instrument with a notorious inferiority complex) and can move in it at something like the pace of a sonata, it is as obvious that he ought to write an opera as that Bruckner, Wagnerian though he was, ought not, and fortunately did not.

The concerto begins with two bars of orchestral introduction which I do not quote, though I shall have to allude to them later. The viola enters with a broad lyric melody in A minor.

Ex. 1.

N.B. &c.

The collision between C sharp in the accompaniment and the C natural in the melody is bold, but it is resolved in the classical way. Nevertheless it is destined to become an unresolved thing in itself and, as such, to be the initial and final motto of the whole work. Accordingly I give this motto here in its tonic position—

Ex. 2.

though its first appearance (during the counterstatement of Ex. 1) is at a high pitch in the course of a sequence that sweeps round a whole enharmonic circle of keys. But the figure soon detaches itself as an individual actor in the drama, and claims derivation from the first two notes of Ex. 1.

What may conveniently be called the second subject (though as my readers know, I have reasons for deprecating the term) first appears in D minor.

Ex. 3.

Its essential feature is the coiling of a sequential figure across the rhythm and across the harmony at every sort of angle. Its transformations are shown in every subsequent cantabile that is not derived from Ex. 1. Another new figure—

Ex. 4.

originates most of the rapid passages in the sequel, and from it, if
we wish to use classical terminology, the development may be said
to begin. Ex. 1 becomes fierce in an entirely new rhythm—

Ex. 5.

which, sometimes reduced to monotone and ragtime—

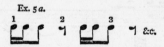

Ex. 5a.

alternates dramatically with developments of Ex. 3, which steadily
grows in beauty and pathos. As the drama unfolds, the motto, Ex. 2,
asserts itself. The last phase of the development is introduced when
the viola makes its exit with Ex. 4, and the orchestra, entering with
Ex. 5 in ominous agitation on the dominant of C sharp minor, rouses
itself to tragic passion, and with grand classical breadth works its
way round to the home dominant, and so to a pathetic slow decline
in which the later figures of the main theme (Ex. 1, the part marked
'N.B.') are heard solemnly augmented.

Over the still reverberating dominant pedal the viola re-enters
with a two-part version of the (unquoted) introductory bars,
expanded into a short cadenza and leading to the return of Ex. 1.
While the viola breaks into a running accompaniment, the melody,
softly delivered in a higher octave, makes a single simple statement
rounded off with a pathetic cadence, and the viola adds a line of
coda alluding to Ex. 3 and ending with the motto, Ex. 2. The whole
movement must convince every listener as a masterpiece of form
in its freedom and precision, besides showing pathos of a high
order.

The middle movement is a lively rondo in E minor with plenty
of ragtime rhythms which, unlike those of jazz, are allowed to
throw the music out of step, so that the composer has now and then
to change the time-signature for one or two bars. The listener need
not worry about these changes; an odd bar of 3/4, 3/8, or 5/8 is
merely a practical necessity for conductor and players; it happens
whenever the composer has found that his groups of 3 or 5 quavers
across his 4-quaver bars will land him on a main beat either too
soon or too late for his whim. Much has been said in favour of jazz;
but jazz, though a composer may be generous in his acknowledgement to it, never kept a movement going like this. A list of themes
must suffice by way of analysis; letters and figures in the quotations
will show a few significant points in the thematic and rhythmic
structure. In general scheme the three movements of this concerto

agree in the common-sense device of reserving the display of the full orchestra for a penultimate stage in which it can make a big climax, leaving room for a coda in which the solo instrument can deliver its final summary.

Here is the main theme of the scherzo, delivered by the viola, with wood-wind echoes.

From its scale-figure (c) many things result; especially a habit of making accompaniments out of bits of scale marching up or down in obstinate little groups of 3, 4, 5, alone, or in 3rds, and always inclined to collide with beat and harmony. The continuation—

arises out of figure (b) and shows how the ragtime refuses to explain itself away. Jazz has often lulled me to sleep by its under-lying monotony; but Walton's rhythms keep me on the alert.

A transition theme, using a figure akin to (b)—

leads to the main theme of the first episode.

The second episode is the beginning of extensive development, starting in F and modulating widely.

Ex. 10.

As the 5-note underlying scale and the semiquaver figures show, it lends itself easily to 'conflation' (as the palaeographist would say) with the other themes; and the transition-theme, Ex. 8, appears conspicuously in the sequel. As in the other movements of this concerto, the orchestra eventually arises in its might, bringing the development to its climax, and leading, at its own leisure, to the final return of the main theme in the tonic. The viola resumes its control in the ensuing compound of recapitulation and coda. The movement ends, according to its nature, with Haydnesque abruptness and Bach-like punctuality.

The lyric qualities of the first movement, and its moderate tempo, have already supplied whatever need this work may have for a slow movement. Yet it is a bold stroke to follow so typical a scherzo by a finale which also begins in a manifestly grotesque style which the bassoon and contrafagotto can do nothing to bowdlerize.

Ex. 11.

But the grotesque is, as Ruskin has defined it, the sublime refracted by terror; and this finale is no joke. In its total effect it is the majestic and pathetic conclusion of a work that is throughout large in all its aspects. The form will explain itself: here is the main figure of the transition theme—

Ex. 12.

and here is the 'second subject'—

Ex. 13.

from which an important figure arises.

Ex. 14.

Later in the movement the viola draws a long line of pathetic cantabile over an ostinato development of the first theme.

Ex. 15.

This cantabile becomes tragically important before the end of the movement.

Another point that may be quoted is the following combination of Ex. 14 with an augmented version of the main figure of Ex. 11.

Ex. 16.

When the orchestra, as in the previous movements, gathers up the threads Ex. 11 reveals itself as a purely majestic subject for a fugal stretto, and the listener will soon become convinced that the total import of the work is that of high tragedy. This is wonderfully realized in the coda. What happens at the end is this: the main theme, Ex. 11, has settled into an ostinato in 9/4 time, and over this the viola brings back the lyric melody of the first movement, Ex. 1, with which the concerto ends, not in the same way as the first movement, but with similar Bach-like punctuality.

There are so few concertos for viola that (even if I happened to know any others) it would be a poor compliment to say this was the finest. Any concerto for viola must be a *tour de force*; but this seems to me to be one of the most important modern concertos for any instrument, and I can see no limits to what may be expected of the tone-poet who could create it.

C. HUBERT H. PARRY

SYMPHONIC VARIATIONS FOR ORCHESTRA

To the pupils of this great English master these symphonic variations will vividly recall the man. To others the work will assuredly reveal him; not perhaps in such detail as his choral works with their unsurpassable truth and depth in the setting of words; but certainly as pure instrumental music can reveal a character that grounded optimism on a brave recognition of facts, that lost all sense of duty and self-sacrifice in the simple pleasure of goodness, and unconsciously destroyed conceit and priggishness as sunlight destroys germs.

Parry never pretended to found or foster a 'distinctively English' style of music—as if it were a smaller thing to be English than to be a musician. He could no more help writing an English style than he could help being a musician. An English style ought, if English music were comparable to English literature, to be the most universal and resourceful of all styles. That is one reason why the best English art can never afford to be provincial and uneducated. An English Berlioz is simply out of the question. The unteachable Berlioz grew up surrounded by artistic logicians and disciplinarians. The unteachable Englishman grows up among people and institutions as chaotically instinctive as himself, with dullness ever at hand as a safe solution of the problems of life. An unlearned British composer trying to write in an English style will, of course, write in the style the average Englishman likes: that is to say, he will write in a style compounded of the religious and theatrical idioms of French, Italian, and Jewish music of the mid-nineteenth century. That compound is English in so far as the genuine recipe for it is not to be found in any other country. The way to attain a true English style is Parry's way: the way of knowledge. That is also the way of instinct; for adequate knowledge allows for instinct and uses it, whereas the man who says too loudly that he 'trusts his instinct' is not always able to discriminate between the nest-building instincts of birds and of mares. Besides, instincts often improve with their surroundings and the resources they have to deal with. An instinct for musical form is more often acquired than innate; yet without it an instinct for melody is mere self-indulgence. For instance, no two melodies could be more unlike each other in all aspects of sentiment and style, except in their innate nobility and simplicity, than the theme of the slow movement of Beethoven's last Quartet (op. 135) and Parry's theme.

Yet the structure of the two themes is nearly identical; viz. a short opening phrase (bar 1), repeated with an added detail (bar 2); then two bars of sequence (bars 3 and 4) rising to a climax (bar 5), which leads to an expanded cadence (bar 6) closing into the beginning of the next variation. No pupil of Parry can forget how directly his teaching aimed at the solid musical facts in all their meaning and capacity. The British composer who merely trusts in what he believes to be instinct, is quite capable of thinking *Home, Sweet Home* a good theme for variations. A theme like this of Parry's is the perfection of English instinct directed to wise purpose by a knowledge which is never irrelevant.

The variations are grouped on a plan of Parry's own, which he has also followed in a remarkable set of pianoforte variations in D minor. The grouping suggests four symphonic movements— an analogy which must not be pressed too far, for it would require a bigger finale, and there would be some difficulty in deciding whether the first two groups should not represent two movements rather than one. If we regard them as the first movement (E minor, followed by E major), we shall have no hesitation in calling the lively C major group the scherzo. The slow movement in A minor (triple time) strikes a tragic note, while the finale is not so much a new movement as a cheerful return to the beginning, in the major mode, with a triumphant amplification of the theme to end with.

The individual variations, as they arise one out of the other, are easily followed from the theme, which I have quoted in its entirety, except as to harmonies. The first gives the melody to the violas, the second to the basses, with a new melody in the winds. At the third the violins come striding in, and soon stir up the orchestra to a rousing measure in the style of a sailor's chanty, with the theme in the bass. Then they settle down to an agitated figure, broken off from the closing notes of a variation, while all the horns and bassoons in unison give a version of the theme. The violin-figure flutters down and away in a beautiful little cadenza for the flute, which leads to the second or tonic-major group of variations (allegretto). This begins with a cheerful duet between a clarinet and a bassoon; then the basses take the clarinet part, while the violas have a version of the original theme. Next, the violins have a soaring figure that reaches and descends from a calm climax into a graceful antiphonal variation—wind answering strings in broken phrases. Soon afterwards the minor mode returns with a version of the theme at half the pace (two bars equal to one of the original) for the solemn quiet mass of brass instruments.

Upon this the scherzo group, in C major, comes dancing in with a playful variation for the flute. The strings follow: then there is a lively game between the strings and the wind, with the theme in staccato syncopations, punctuated by a snapping figure in the wood-wind. The tackling (if a Rugby technicality be admissible at Eton) is excellent. The trumpets next have their say; after which the strings and drums stir up a whirlwind, which finally settles down into a long shake for the clarinets (a very difficult shake too), while the strings have a slow and broken pizzicato version of the theme.

The shake changes towards A minor, and suddenly the slow-movement group bursts in with tragic pomp. It contains four powerful variations, the last of which is expanded, with an increase of pace, to a dramatic climax. The solemn catastrophic collapse from this leads to nothing more than a perfectly nonchalant return to a version of the original theme in the original tempo, but in the tonic major. A pupil of Parry can almost hear his laugh as he asks, 'What's old Tchaikovsky making all this fuss about?' Then the clarinets start a merry variation at twice the pace. The violins come running in, and soon, with but little expansion, the work marches to a brilliant close in terms of its own theme— spacious, adequate, and final—with no preaching or tub-thumping to make it seem too small for all that has been devoted to it. Not only the battle of Waterloo was won upon the playing-fields of Eton, but this battle against the Philistines also.

'OVERTURE TO AN UNWRITTEN TRAGEDY'

I hope that the public will come to agree with me in gratitude to Sir Adrian Boult for rediscovering one of the finest works of my beloved master, Hubert Parry. I heard its first performance in the 'nineties, and I confess with shame that I have only now studied the score. Yet for me these thirty-odd years of neglect have resulted in showing me this masterpiece in lights which I should otherwise have missed. The score recalls vividly to me many impressions of its first performance; amongst others, that it was marked by the perfunctory efficiency which never rises beyond the level of that skill in sight-reading for which British musicians were already famous in the days of Wagner. I do not remember the names of either orchestra or conductor; the hall was St. James's,[1] and I am not sure that the Queen's Hall had then been opened. At that time I fiercely resented the slightest criticism of my beloved master's work; and when one of Parry's most loyal and distin-guished colleagues remarked to me, 'I don't think the coda quite

[1] No; an obliging reader has kindly sent me the programme of the occasion; it was at the Queen's Hall.

comes off', I saw no future for British music except to be stifled in wet blankets by its friends. Curiously enough, I now have a strong impression that the printed score has a different end from that which I heard then. I can trust none of these memories; so many of them drift into memories of later reflections on the subject; but I am almost certain that the resigned pathos of the coda, with its major mode, was retained to the end, and that the overture died away without a final outburst of energy.

It is surprising that Ex. 3, the main theme of the Allegro, is the only one that I remember, and that my memory of it is quite exact for the first bar and a half, that is, for the whole identifying clause. Two essential features of it are new to me, and from this I infer that the performance was as uncomprehending as the programme notes. The violent scoring of these shattering rhythms in massed chords, and the fierce accents in unexpected places, these are features that I surely would have remembered if the performance had done justice to them; and I cannot imagine that they are points added after revision.

Like Brahms's Tragic Overture, the influence of which it shows at no cost to its own independence, Parry's overture puzzled every one who believed that the word 'tragic' applies primarily to disasters that demand the attention of the police and secondarily to stage dramas in which the final curtain falls on the violent death of one or more persons who could never have been happy under any conceivable circumstances. The writer of those programme notes in the 'nineties seemed puzzled by the considerable differences between this *Overture to an Unwritten Tragedy* and the finale of Tchaikovsky's Pathetic Symphony. He quoted one passage in bustling semiquavers, and said, 'this, at all events, seems gay'. I have only a vague recollection of the 'look of the page' to help me to identify the 'gay' passage. It almost certainly was not Ex. 6; and the development opens with a quite mysterious semiquaver passage which recalls to me the 'look' of the quotation, but which is not thematic at all and which introduces, with appropriate dramatic suspense, one of the most pathetic parts of the whole work. Let no one imagine that those English composers of the 'nineties whom our iconoclasts dubbed 'proud academics' were a mutual admiration society that grew rich in the production of 'best sellers'. In the 'nineties anything like solid knowledge of musical composition was quite as much a persecuted heresy as it has been since; and the devotion of our 'proud academics' to the service of music was utterly unalloyed with any selfish aims or vanities.

Parry's overture begins with an introduction on a large scale. In Ex. 1 the bass and inner parts comprise in their first three notes a figure (*a*) which may be traced in many of the later themes—

Ex. 1.

For instance, out of that figure arises a contrasted cantabile beginning thus in F major—

Ex. 2.

and mounting in sequences to a tremendous climax which culminates in the fierce main theme of the allegro energico.

Ex. 3.

From this point the overture moves rapidly, instantly proceeding to a transition theme—

Ex. 4.

which rises to a great height of passion before subsiding pathetically, with an allusion to Ex. 1, figure (b), and closing into the second group.

The second group begins with a consolatory cantabile in
C major—

Ex. 5.

the counterstatement of which leads to an animato theme—

Ex. 6.

which works up to a climax marked by a cadence theme—

Ex. 7.

This repeats itself with the usual cadential emphasis, and, after
another noble climax, leads to a die-away end.

The final close is interrupted by a change of harmony, and the
development begins with mysterious whisperings in the violins
(is this the Victorian analyst's 'note of gaiety'?), which lead to a
pathetic working-up of the inner figure (a) of Ex. 1, in the present
tempo. The general tendency of the development is to assimilate
the material of the introduction to the tempo and style of the
allegro. Thus, after a short crescendo has led to an outburst of
Ex. 3, the next event is a development of Ex. 2, which now leads
to the recapitulation by a process similar to, but shorter than,
that with which it led to the allegro.

The recapitulation is compressed but regular, giving in the
tonic major almost the whole transition and the whole second
group. But the cadence theme (Ex. 7), instead of leading to a
climax and a die-away, leads to a dramatic catastrophe marked
by a pause—

Ex. 8.

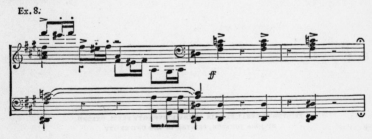

and followed (as the example indicates) by a deeply pathetic new development of figure (*b*) and other features of the introduction. Then the coda settles to a quiet *Verklärung* (transfiguration) suggestive (but not more than suggestive) of Ex. 5. But the climax that follows is concerned with the energetic themes, Exx. 3 and 7; and the final note of the overture, though solemn and in the major mode, is not that of peace, but of confidence that the battles which yet must come are worth fighting even if the only victory is death.

Parry's title for this noble work happily forbids us to find for it any more definite programme.

PRINTED IN GREAT BRITAIN AT THE UNIVERSITY PRESS, OXFORD
BY JOHN JOHNSON, PRINTER TO THE UNIVERSITY